Horst Hegewald-Kawich

The German Shepherd Dog

Expert advice on training, care, and nutrition

Color photos by Monika Wegler and drawings by György Jankovics

Consulting Editor:
  Matthew M. Vriends, Ph.D.

BARRON'S

Contents

Inside cover: A splendid example of a female German shepherd dog (Indy von der Kupferschale). With a powerful bound, this bundle of energy crosses to the opposite bank of the stream.

If you see to it that your dog is properly cared for and trained from the beginning, you will have no problems later.

Preface

The German shepherd dog has almost attained the status of legend. Renowned for its intelligence, courage, strength, and good character, it is one of the most popular dog breeds in the world. It has earned a worldwide reputation for its qualities as a fearless guard dog, police dog, and working dog. Less well known, however, are the engaging qualities that make the German shepherd dog such a devoted companion.

In this pet owner's manual, dog expert Horst Hegewald-Kawich tells you everything you need to know about keeping a German shepherd dog. He gives sound advice on choosing and buying a puppy, helping it adjust to your household, and meeting its nutritional needs. On the basis of long years of experience in dealing with German shepherd dogs, he recommends a firm, consistent approach to training, tells you what to do if your pet becomes ill, and outlines a responsible breeding program. The author places special emphasis on the need to keep this work-loving dog occupied. Dogs that have too little to do often become severely disturbed, and may become dangerous.

On the HOW-TO pages: The topics covered are training, physical fitness, grooming, and health. Exercises are described, and important procedures are explained step by step. Informative drawings by György Jankovics bring the text to life. The handsome full-color photos by Monika Wegler, a well-known photographer of animals, provide lively images of this original, "rugged" breed.

*Please read the
"Important Note"
on page 63.*

3

Understanding German Shepherd Dogs

The German shepherd dog is the one breed that most closely resembles the common ancestor of all canines—the wolf; however, that is no reason to fear it.

A Dog That Far Exceeds Its Reputation

The German shepherd dog has excellent qualities and traits of character: It is intelligent and high-spirited, radiates a rugged kind of strength, exhibits keen alertness, and defends its owner and his or her property with courage and tenacity. At the same time, it displays self-confidence, likes children, and is steady and unexcitable. Given appropriate care, it is easy to handle and train. It loves to work and can be employed in a variety of ways—as a guard dog, police dog, working dog, or companion dog. Each year, German shepherd dogs find hundreds of avalanche victims and people buried under debris. They help police find narcotics, explosives, or concealed bodies. They lead the blind, assist the handicapped, and are still employed as herding dogs, their original "profession."

Some people, however, are uneasy when they encounter a German shepherd dog. Is this the "Little Red Riding Hood and the Big Bad Wolf" syndrome," instilled in us from earliest childhood and reinforced by headlines such as "German Shepherd Dog Mauls Child?" Or is it the "keep away" behavior of some German shepherd dog owners when out in public or engaged in training? In any event, it is not the dog's fault that its reputation has suffered; in most cases, a human is at fault. Nevertheless, the German shepherd dog is still is one of the most popular dog breeds in the world.

A Herding Dog at Heart

If you have never seen a German shepherd dog engaged in its original work as a herder, try to make up for that as quickly as possible. You will be enraptured! Every year, usually in southern Germany, the Verein für Deutsche Schäferhunde (German Shepherd Dog Society) holds a national livestock herding competition (see Useful Addresses, page 62, for the address in the United States). There you will see the top professional herdsmen with their German shepherd dogs, working with the flocks.

The German shepherd dog has at heart remained a herder, although today it is rarely to be found engaged in this activity. Instead, it conscientiously guards house and yard, keeps an eye on children or other pets that live in the same household, and—lacking a herd of cattle or sheep to protect—untiringly circles around its "human flock" when out for a walk.

A Dog That Needs Challenges

The impressive talents of the German shepherd dog appear to reach their highest potential only if the dog has

German shepherd dogs are not afraid of water—just the opposite! On hot days they will gladly submerge themselves up to their neck ruff.

This German shepherd dog spends as much as 12 hours a day, covering enormous distances, guiding its flock.

been carefully bred and if its owner then takes proper care of it and trains it with consistency. In addition, the dog has to be kept busy, since its intelligence, energy, and desire to work need to be properly channeled (see page 32).

Dogs that are "underemployed," frequently become a problem for their owner and their environment. These dogs are mentally unstable, and they can become dangerous.

The Ancestors of the German Shepherd Dog

As early as the year 37 B.C., the Roman scholar and encyclopedist Marcus Terentius Varo (116–27 B.C.) warned farmers against purchasing dogs from butchers or hunters to guard their herds of sheep or cattle. Aware of the special bent of herding dogs, he assumed that a "butcher's dog" would be more apt to attack the stock than to protect it, and that a hunter's dog would prefer to chase the animals.

These chronicles prove that livestock dogs have been used by shepherds to protect their flocks for at least 2,000 years, and probably even longer. In those days, however, and until the sixteenth century, the dogs used for that purpose were big, heavy animals, capable of "throttling" wolves and protecting the groups of sheep or cattle from packs of thieves of every description. Herd dogs were described as "large mean dogs with shaggy, curly hair."

Late Medieval Times

As population density rapidly increased, people began to employ medium-sized, quick-moving herding dogs. Such animals, known in those days as "dung-barkers," had long been

Hektor Linksrhein, under the name Horand von Grafrath, was the first entry in the stud book of the German Shepherd Dog Society.

kept by farmers as estate guard dogs.

Sheepherders started breeding and selecting only those dogs that could work in all kinds of weather, those that were trainable and had enormous powers of endurance. Also, they had to have a certain inclination to bite, since, after all, they were supposed to control the herds. Wild biters that injured the flocks were obviously undesirable. The herding dog's coat, which originally was long, shaggy, and matted, offered protection against the teeth of wolves. As humans increasingly conquered new living space and drove the wolves back, they came to prefer herding dogs with a shorter, though still relatively shaggy, coat. By this time, there was great variety in the external appearance of herder dogs. There were dogs with erect, folded, and drooping ears, straight-haired dogs, shaggy-haired dogs, and curly-haired dogs with either curly tails or drooping tails. They came in a wide range of colors as well. With this large supply of "herding dog material," breeders set about developing a straight-haired herder with pointed ears and a drooping tail.

The Beginning of Selective Breeding

In 1899, Captain of Cavalry Max von Stephanitz was introduced to Hektor Linksrhein, a male shepherd dog, by his friend Arthur Meyer, who had seen it at a show. The dog, which came from the von Wachsmuth kennel, belonged to Friedrich Sparwasser, a Frankfurt breeder of shepherd dogs. Stephanitz bought this dog because he was convinced that it possessed all the prerequisites for attaining the breeding goal he had set himself—a German shepherd dog. He renamed the dog Horand von Grafrath and entered him as Number 1 in the newly established stud book of the

"Verein für Deutsche Schäferhunde" (German Shepherd Dog Society), founded in April 1899, thus making him the ancestor of all German shepherd dogs.

Becoming fashionable: Under the leadership of Max von Stephanitz as founder and president of the German Shepherd Dog Club, the breeding of German shepherd dogs began a meteoric rise. By 1924 almost 50,000 dogs were listed in the stud book. At this time, however, a certain deterioration of character in the dogs became apparent, and critics even began to warn against excessive angulation of the hindquarters (see page 11). Breeding programs no longer focused on working value alone, but began to reflect on outward appearance as well. The dog was no longer in as much demand as a herder, because farming was on the rise and sheep raising continued to decline. Dogs were literally torn from the breeders' hands. German shepherd dogs were in demand everywhere in Europe. In addition, many dogs (as is still true today) were offered for sale not only through the German Shepherd Dog Society, but by unreliable breeders as well.

The road to recovery: Only the introduction of, and rigorous adherence to, regulations governing inspection and selection of animals suitable for breeding, in combination with an emphasis on functional characteristics, brought about an improvement in the German shepherd dog's traits. In Germany, there still exists a panel of judges who assess a dog's fitness for breeding, using the requirements set forth in the breed standard. It is up to this panel to decide whether a dog is barred from breeding altogether, has only limited suitability, or is recommended for proper breeding.

Until World War II, the breed was continuously improved by conscientious breeders, although—as was the case with all other dog breeds—more attention was still being paid to external "beautification," rather than to traits of character.

Exploitation in the field: By this time, the manifold talents of the German shepherd dog had become apparent, and during World War II most of the best breeding material was conscripted for active duty in war work as guard dogs, medical corps dogs, or messenger dogs. The German shepherd dog—a misused, faithful friend—bled to death on every front of the unfortunate war.

New attempts at breeding: When the war was over, the breeding of German shepherd dogs was almost nonexistent. The best of the dogs were dead or in the hands of the Allies; American soldiers took many German shepherd dogs home with them. These dogs provided the core of what is now a first-rate line of German shepherd dogs in the United States. German breeders had to start over from scratch. Later, following the division of Germany into East and West, each part of the country continued its breeding program without any mutual exchange of breeding material. For more than 40 years, two genetically screened populations of the same breed had an opportunity to develop side by side.

The German Shepherd Dog

This is a dog of superlatives, as far as its intelligence, ability to be trained and handled, willingness to work, and physical agility are concerned. The German shepherd dog ranks as one of the most popular dog breeds in the world. The breed standard specifies a graceful gait, stiff, thick, flat, coarse hair, with a thick undercoat and straight, close-fitting hair on top. The most common colors are black or black saddle with tan, gold, or gray markings.

A black and tan long-haired male.

Black long-haired female and black and tan short-haired male.

Standard: Black and tan short-haired male from the kennel Zack von der Mühltalleiten.

A "wolf-gray" short-haired male from the kennel "Falk von Hopfengut."

The present-day German shepherd dog developed from "old German" herding dogs similar to this one.

A six-week-old short-haired puppy.

The Breed Standard

The breed standard describes the way an ideal representative of a breed looks. It is drawn up in the country of origin of the breed and deposited with the parent organization for that country's dog clubs (in the United States, the American Kennel Club, or AKC; see Useful Addresses, page 62). The national parent organization transmits the actual breed standard to its member organizations, so that uniform judging criteria for the given dog breed are available.

A brief description of the way an ideal representative of the German shepherd dog is supposed to look follows.

General appearance: The German shepherd dog is robust, supple, and well muscled. A gently sloping line runs from the tips of the ears over the back to the tip of the tail, without a break. The body seems slightly elongated; that is, the torso is somewhat longer than the height at the withers.

Character: Well-balanced, intelligent, confident, even-tempered, and good-natured; yet also hard-working, courageous, aggressive, and tough, if the situation requires. The dog can be both devoted companion and fearless guardian.

Size and weight: The German shepherd dog is one of the medium-sized breeds. The height at the withers is 24 to 26 inches (63–64 cm) for adult males and 22 to 24 inches (58–59 cm) for females. For both males and females, the weight for the adult dog is about 70.5 pounds (32 kg). Under the Canadian standard, 75 to 85 pounds (34–38.5 kg) for the adult dog, and 60 to 70 pounds (27.2–31.8 kg) for the bitch.

Head: In proportion with the dog's body clear-cut, and fairly broad between the ears. The forehead is only moderately domed. The upper head accounts for about half of the overall head length. The nose is black, the muzzle straight.

Teeth: In the required scissors bite, the incisors meet in a scissor bite. The puppy has 28 teeth, the adult dog 42 (20 in the upper jaw and 22 in the lower).

Ears: Medium-sized, broad at the base, and set high on the head. They end in a point and, along with the outer ear, open toward the front. The ears of young dogs sometimes hang until the sixth month or later.

Eyes: They should be dark, almond-shaped, and slightly slanting, not protruding. They have an alert, highly intelligent, and self-assured expression.

Neck: Fairly long and well muscled, without loose folds of skin on the throat. When the dog is at attention or excited, seven cervical vertebrae lift the neck to an erect position; at other times, it typically is carried level.

Top line: It commences at the tips of the ears and runs without break or interruption, gently sloping, over the back to the tip of the tail.

Well bred: a serviceable dog with a gently sloping back line.

Withers: High and very pronounced. When the dog is standing, they are the highest point on its back.

Back: Straight, powerfully muscled, and without sag or roach (convex curvature or arch of the back toward the rear). It is supported by 13 dorsal vertebrae. The loins are broad and strong; the seven lumbar vertebrae are firmly linked together.

Croup: The extension of the spine should slope gradually. Too level or flat a croup prevents proper functioning of the hindquarter, which must be able to reach well under the body.

Tail: It is made up of 18 to 23 vertebrae. Its bony portion extends at least to the hock and should not be curled forward beyond the middle of the rear metatarsus. When the dog is at rest, the tail hangs in a slight curve. When the dog is excited or in motion, the tail should never be lifted beyond a line at right angles with the line of the back.

Bottom line: It begins at the neck and runs over the upper and lower chest, sloping up slightly toward the rear. The abdomen is firmly held and only moderately tucked up in the loin. The chest must be well filled and capacious. The relationship between height at the withers and body length is expressed as a ratio of 9 to 10; that is, a dog 24 inches (60 cm) high should be roughly 26 inches (67 cm) long.

The lower chest is as long as possible. The ribs are slightly domed. The depth of the chest should not exceed half of the height at the withers.

Forequarters: The shoulder blades are long and placed at an oblique angle, laid on flat and not placed forward. The upper arm is well muscled and attached at about a right angle. The forelegs are straight, viewed from all sides. The pasterns are strong and not too steep; the elbows are neither wide apart nor sloping.

"Overstyled" and bred only for visual appeal: a dog with a steeply sloping back line that leads to joint problems.

Hindquarters: Haunches are broad and powerfully muscled. Upper thighs are fairly long and set at almost a right angle to the lower thighs. Ankle and rear metatarsus are strong and tightly articulated. The dog should stand with its weight slightly on the hind limbs.

Feet: They are rounded and short, with the toes compact and well arched. The pads of the feet are thick and firm. The nails are dark in color, short, and strong.

Coat: Only short hair is allowed, consisting of an outer (top) coat and a thick inner- or undercoat. The outer coat is dense and of medium length; the hairs are stiff, thick, flat, and coarse, breeching near the thighs. Hair length varies.

Coat color: Black with brown markings, tan or light gray with black and dark brown saddle. Small white markings on the chest or inside of the legs are permissible. Other colors are solid black, iron gray, and brown-gray. The undercoat is faintly colored. The final color of a puppy can be determined only after the outer coat has come in.

Choosing and Buying a German Shepherd Dog

Before you buy a German shepherd dog, take time to think through all the consequences of such an acquisition. Ask yourself whether you and your family can offer the dog a good home and the proper care. You also need to be aware that the average life span of a German shepherd is 12 years. During this entire time, you are responsible for the well-being of your pet.

Will a German Shepherd Dog Suit Your Lifestyle?

The following questions are intended to help you decide whether to buy a German shepherd dog:
• As far as both your career and your private life are concerned, are you able to make plans over a period of about 12 years?
• Will your landlord (if you have one) allow you to keep a pet, according to the terms of your lease?
• Can you offer the dog enough room and, if at all possible, a yard? German shepherd dogs are not meant to be exclusively indoor pets.
• Are you prepared to take two to three long walks a day with your dog, even in bad weather?
• Can you guarantee that the dog will not be left alone for longer than three hours during the day?
• Do you have the requisite time to teach your dog the basics, give it advanced training later on, or engage in athletic activities with it?
• Are you willing to plan your vacations so that you can take your dog

along? If not, is there someone familiar to the dog who will take care of it when you are away or sick? Not all dogs can tolerate being boarded.
• Are you prepared to pay for your dog's food, grooming expenses, and veterinary costs, as well as a dog license and a liability insurance policy?
• Are all the members of your family in agreement about the purchase of a German shepherd dog?
• Is anyone in your family allergic to dog hair? If you are uncertain, consult a physician before buying a dog.

Male or Female?

Whether you acquire a male or a female depends primarily on your personal preference. In my experience, there are no differences in character and temperament—a male is just as affectionate as a female.

The male has a more imposing outward appearance than the female, but is more inclined to get into scuffles with other males. On walks, he marks his territory with urine more frequently. If he picks up the scent of a female dog in heat, he leaves his scent marks at every opportunity.

The female comes into heat, or estrus, twice a year. Each cycle is accompanied by bleeding, which may last as long as 20 days (see the chapter on breeding, beginning on page 54). During this time the female, or bitch, is sometimes more restless than usual. If you do not want unplanned offspring, make sure that no male dog

Which one of us is stronger? These puppies are learning to estimate their strength while having fun tugging on a piece of rope.

After retrieving the ball, this dog willingly lets go of it to prepare for the next toss.

has a chance to come near during this period.

Puppy or Adult?

Choosing a puppy has definite advantages. You can have a direct influence on the dog's developmental phases by training it properly and fostering its potential (see Training Your Puppy, page 26). While rearing the puppy, however, you need plenty of time, patience, and firmness.

My tip: Before acquiring a puppy, gather information about dog training—unintentional mistakes in care and training can cause behavioral disturbances and such German shepherd dogs often become dangerous later.

With an adult dog, the process of physical development is already complete, and its character has already been molded. From these standpoints, you will have to do less work with your pet at first. Keep in mind, however, that a change of ownership, new surroundings, and unfamiliar people can rattle the dog at first. You need to show plenty of understanding for your pet.

How to Find a Reputable Breeder

Gather information from the American Kennel Club, the parent organization for all breed clubs in the United States. Also consult the German Shepherd Club of America (see Useful Addresses, page 62). They can give you the addresses of breeders who are members of these clubs and adhere to strict breeding regulations. Visit as many breeders as you can so that you can compare the animals themselves as well as the conditions in which they are kept. Don't be put off by having to make long trips to do this. The important thing is to get a physically and mentally healthy puppy. With small

breeders, the dogs live with the family. They are accustomed to people and may even be housebroken before they leave their first homes. Pups raised by large breeders, on the other hand, are often shy and may even be behaviorally disturbed because they have had little contact with humans. Do not buy your dog from a kennel that has all breeds, either. In most cases, such kennels are little more than large collections of dogs cared for by too few and not very knowledgeable people, whose main interest is not dogs, but profit. Sick animals are fairly common. Be especially cautious about special offers in the newspaper. My advice is to search out a breeder who breeds nothing but German shepherd dogs and who raises the animals in a manner suitable to this breed.

What to look for:
• Make sure the facility is kept clean, and the breeding animals are in perfect condition and well cared for.
• The breeder should be affectionate in his or her dealings with the dogs. The mother dog, or dam, and her puppies should display no fear of the breeder or of you.
• The puppies should be allowed inside the breeder's house, in order to become accustomed to visitors and household noises by the time they go to new homes.
• The breeder should ask questions about your personal circumstances and the puppy's new living conditions. This "curiosity" speaks well for the breeder; it indicates that he or she feels responsible for the puppies' future.

Do not buy if:
• you are not allowed to take a look at the facilities;
• the puppies are growing up in a cage, far from the breeder's living quarters;
• the breeder uses more than two breeding bitches or several dog breeds in his or her breeding program. Such

For a child, a dog is both a playmate and a partner. Through the dog, the child learns to behave responsibly and independently. A German shepherd dog with a good character is usually very gentle with children.

14

people have little time to pay attention to puppies during the critical imprinting phases (see page 20). Behavioral disturbances often are programmed into the young animals right from the start.

Caution: As stated before, beware of dogs sold through an ad in the newspaper, since "puppy mills" frequently advertise their puppies for sale in this way. If you buy a puppy out of pity, you are only lending support to the underhanded practices of people who unscrupulously exploit animals.

The Certificate of Origin

This document—the pedigree—shows the puppy's parentage. The German Shepherd Club of America has strong recommendations about, for example, which colors of German shepherd dogs should be mated together. Your potential pup's pedigree should show that these color-breeding recommendations have been followed. The pedigree should also show any champions or obedience title holders in your prospective pup's ancestry.

The American Kennel Club registration certificate confirms that the puppy is purebred, with its mother (dam) and father (sire) both registered German shepherd dogs. You should also receive application forms to forward to the AKC in order to register this puppy, if you buy it, in your name.

Examine the dog's pedigree papers thoroughly. In the United States and various other countries, these pedigree papers will contain not only the dog's ancestry back to the great-great-grandparents but also the dog's identification number. This number is tattooed on the puppy on the inside of the dog's left leg, the groin, or the inside of the ear when it is about eight weeks old, and any German shepherd dog without this tattooed number will not be registered as a

Puppies engaged in socialization play—now up, now down.

purebred. In the United States, the owner's Social Security number is often used as identification for mixed-breed dogs; in the case of pedigreed German shepherd dogs, the dog's American Kennel Club registration number is used. No judge may penalize or disqualify a dog because of a tattoo. With a purebred German shepherd dog, you can be fairly sure of getting what you expect to get. With one that is not purebred, you should be braced for the unexpected!

Immunization

Not only are inoculations against an array of harmful or potentially fatal diseases a pivotal part of your German shepherd dog's preventive health plan, but in most places some of these illness-fighting vaccinations are also required by law!

Your puppy may have had its first immunizations at about six weeks of age while still at the breeder's. These initial shots were vaccinations for distemper and measles and possibly for parvovirus, canine hepatitis, leptospirosis, parainfluenza, coronavirus, and bordetella (see Preventive Care and Diseases, beginning on page 48).

The vaccination record should be a part of the permanent paperwork you obtain when you purchase a puppy or an adult dog. Your pet's veterinarian needs to know what vaccinations (or other treatments) your dog received before you became its owner. This complete accounting of what has been done to and for your dog will form the foundation of your pet's health records, which should be kept current and accurate throughout the life of the dog.

Usually, the breeder will have wormed the puppies before selling them (see page 48). Ask how often and with what preparations the puppy was wormed. Before buying the puppy, have a veterinarian examine it thoroughly once more.

The Contract of Sale

When you buy a dog, it is essential to conclude a contract of sale. It provides both the buyer and the seller with legal safeguards. If legal disputes arise, the contract of sale will be useful. It should contain the following:
• your address and telephone number as well as those of the breeder;
• the puppy's name, sex, date of birth, AKC registration number, and possibly the tattoo number;
• the price paid for the puppy;
• the date on which the puppy changed hands.

Choosing a Puppy

Puppies between eight and 10 weeks old are the easiest to get settled in new surroundings, and you can get an early start on training during the socialization phase (see HOW-TO: Training Your Puppy, page 26). Several weeks before the puppies will be ready to go to new homes, get acquainted with them at the breeder's, then visit them on a frequent basis to observe them for extended periods at play and at mealtimes. A reputable breeder will welcome your interest and help you pick out a puppy. He or she can tell you which dog has the particular traits you are looking for. You yourself can check the state of the puppy's healthy by noting the following:
• A healthy puppy is lively and playful.
• It is well nourished (neither too fat nor too thin).
• It comes up to you inquisitively and trustingly.
• Its coat is clean and glossy; it should not smell of feces or urine.
• Its eyes and nose are free of discharges; its ears are clean.
• In a male puppy, both testicles should be palpable. Do not press on them with force, however; instead, have the breeder help you make your inspection.

Before pick-up day, do the following:
• A few days ahead of time, bring a blanket to the breeder, so that it will pick up the smell of the kennel. It will make the puppy's separation from its mother and siblings easier and help it feel at home in its new surroundings.
• Ask the breeder what the puppy is being fed, since it usually will react to abrupt changes in its diet by developing gastrointestinal upsets.
• Make an appointment with the veterinarian for the second day after your puppy's arrival, to have your new pet thoroughly examined.

Accommodations for Your Dog

Taking proper care of a dog also means that the dog is allowed to spend time where its "people" live.

A German shepherd puppy will have no difficulty getting used to other pets; be cautious with small animals such as guinea pigs, hamsters, and parakeets, however, as the dog will consider them prey. Keep these animals securely caged at all times.

So what if he's bigger? This female basset hound is giving the male German shepherd dog the brush-off.

Indoor sleeping place: The dog needs a dry, draft-free spot in your house or apartment, a place from which it has an adequate overview of its "family." It can retreat to that spot whenever it wants peace and quiet and should not be disturbed by children at such times. You can provide a dog basket to put the puppy in; a large selection of dog baskets is available in pet stores. You also can give the dog a soft, washable blanket to lie on.

My tip: Dogs love to lie in a spot some distance off the ground. With a little know-how, you can build a small platform out of wood and set the dog's blanket or basket on top of it.

An outdoor run: If you have a yard, you also can keep your dog there a few hours each day, inside a closed-in area (run) that contains a doghouse. During the initial period, however, the puppy should stay inside your home exclusively. Then gradually get it used to being in the outdoor run.

Important: Keeping your active German shepherd dog chained is inappropriate, even if the chain is long and allows the dog to move around.

Essential Equipment

Before you bring your puppy home, you should have all its equipment and accessories ready.

Collar: The collar for your new puppy should be adjustable and designed to grow along with your pet. Simple collars made of leather or nylon are ideal. For adult dogs, chain collars or collars made of soft leather are tried-and-true choices, although some experts believe that leather is not such a good choice because moisture, heat, and cold will damage the leather, and it will take on an unpleasant odor after a while. Spiked collars should be used only for training, and then only for short periods of time with particularly temperamental and recalcitrant dogs.

Address tag: In case your pet should ever run away, you should purchase a small leather holder or waterproof cylinder that is designed to hold an address. They can be fastened to your dog's collar. You also can have your phone number or address engraved on the collar.

Leash: The leash for the puppy should be made of leather, approximately 6.5 feet (2 m) in length, and equipped with a secure snap hook. Chain-link leashes are not suitable until the dog has mastered leash training (see HOW-TO: Training Your Puppy, page 27), as it could damage its teeth by biting on the chain. If you want to do a lot of tracking work, you need a lightweight leather leash 33 feet (10 m) long, even for a puppy. For an older dog, a leather leash about 3 to 6.5 feet (1–2 m) long, equipped with a hand loop and a clasp hook is a good choice.

Coat care: Buy a brush with hard bristles, a dog comb with fine and coarse teeth, a dog brush (currycomb), and a dust comb or flea comb (see HOW-TO: Grooming, page 46).

Food and water dishes: These have to be sturdy, skidproof, and easy to clean. I recommend the practical bowls made  of high-grade steel, attached to a pole so that their height can be adjusted. For water, you also can use a ceramic bowl that will keep the water fresh for a long time.

Toys: In order to keep your dog occupied and to give it something to chew on, toys are essential. Pet stores have a large assortment available. The toy should not be capable of injuring the dog, nor should it be made of a material that will splinter. Old shoes are *not* suitable, because the dog cannot distinguish between an old and a new shoe! Don't use rocks or small sticks; rocks will damage the dog's teeth and sticks might injure its mouth. You can throw a tennis ball or a hard rubber ball to foster your pet's instinct to pursue quarry. This activity will be important in subsequent training.

Dried pieces of rawhide about 4 inches (10 cm) long are healthy toys for chewing. Never give such items to your dog before you feed it, however, and be sure to include the amount consumed in your pet's daily food ration, to keep the dog from becoming overweight.

Acclimation and Daily Routine

The time has come; you can pick up your puppy at the breeder's. Make an appointment, since the puppy should not eat anything during the hours before the trip, to keep it from throwing up during the ride.

Making Your Home Safe for Your Dog

Even before you bring your pup home, be aware of possible dangers in your home and take steps to correct or eliminate them.

The Trip Home

It is best to bring your puppy home in a car, and to have a second person accompany you. Take along a towel, a roll of paper towels, a collar, a leash, a bowl, fresh water, and some dry food. Put the puppy's collar on it; then set it on the floor of the car, just in front of the passenger seat, on top of the blanket you gave the breeder ahead of time. During the trip, do not let the dog have an opportunity to look out of the window. The sight of the landscape "flying by" can upset its stomach. You should sit on the passenger seat, to calm the puppy down, if necessary.

On longer car trips you need to take a short break every hour or so in order to let the dog run around—on leash— so it has a chance to do its business and to get some exercise. Then give it fresh water to drink and a small amount of the dry food to eat.

The First Hours in Its New Home

Everything is strange and new to the little puppy, and after the great excitement of the trip, it needs peace and quiet. The other members of the family should not immediately make a beeline for the new arrival. Ask friends and relatives who also want to admire the puppy to be patient and to wait a few days before visiting.

Careful acclimation: Carry the puppy, along with its blanket, to the place you have designated for it. Set out water and the puppy's customary food. After it has eaten, take it outside, so that it can answer nature's call. Then let it run around indoors and get its bearings. When it lies down,

A puppy needs a place of its own, where it can always find its special blanket.

exhausted, carry it back to its blanket and let it sleep.

Choosing a name: By the time the puppy arrives, you should have settled on a name for it. Always use its name in connection with something positive—while you are petting it, for example. Then it will quickly react to its name.

The First Nights at Home

Put the puppy, with its blanket, next to your bed. Or, you can sleep for a few nights in the room in which you want it to stay. That way you can pet it reassuringly when it whimpers because it misses its mother and littermates, or you can quickly carry it outside when it is restless and has to "go" (see Housebreaking, page 26). A good solution for the first two or three weeks is a sleeping basket with sides high enough that the puppy cannot climb out of it so easily. Every day, move the basket a little closer to your bedroom door. In this way, you will gradually get the dog used to sleeping alone. During the first few weeks, you will need to get up at night to take your puppy outdoors,

Caught—before it can get away from its mother.

as its bladder is still too small to make it through the entire night.

My tip: Be sure you don't take the puppy into your own bed out of sympathy. Once you have allowed it to sleep there, it will want to do so from then on—even as a full-grown dog—and by then it will weigh more than 66 pounds (30 kg)!

The Puppy's Developmental Phases

The first eight weeks: The imprinting phases begin at the age of about two to three weeks. The puppy learns its first lessons in social behavior from its mother and littermates; then it has to imprint to humans as well. A good breeder will promote extensive contact at this time.

Ninth to twelfth weeks: During this socialization phase the puppies learn to respect the authority of the adult dogs and the rules that apply in the pack. Your puppy now will view you and your family as its "pack." It will test you to see how far it can go. Playing together is very important. It reinforces the bond between owner and pet. For this reason, the "alpha male or female" in particular needs to set aside several hours a day for the puppy during the first few weeks. The puppy also needs to play with other dogs, however, to learn canine social behavior. Some dog clubs and other organizations offer so-called imprinting play sessions for that purpose (see Useful Addresses, page 62).

Twelfth to twentieth weeks: During this time, the puppy is growing into a young dog. This is the most important, as well as the most vulnerable, phase in the dog's life, so far as the development of its bond to its human owner and its social behavior toward other dogs are concerned. Everything the dog experiences at this stage, whether positive or negative, becomes deeply rooted in its

Puppies love to lie next to their mother.

life. Whatever your pet fails to experience because you lack time for it cannot be derived from later experience.

From the sixth month on: The phases that will decisively influence the rest of your dog's life are now behind it. Before your pet is an adult dog—that is at the age of about one year—you still have to weather its "puberty," a stage at which it will challenge quite a few of your rules. By remaining firm and consistent, however, you will get over this hurdle as well.

Building Trust

If you and your pet are to live together in harmony, it is essential that the dog come to trust you.

Trust in you: Without your pet's trust, you can neither teach it the fundamentals of obedience, give it advanced training later, nor engage in athletic activities with it. You must never jeopar-

dize this relationship of trust by inconsistent behavior, use of improper force, or an outburst of temper. Don't attempt to train your dog when you are impatient or in a bad mood. Your behavior needs to be predictable. Always use the same voice signals to tell your pet what you want of it or what is off-limits. Don't let it get away with behavior one day that you punish it for the next. Achieve your objectives patiently; otherwise, the puppy will take advantage of your inconsistency.

Trust in its environment: Slowly begin to build the puppy's trust in the world around it. During the first few weeks, don't make long excursions to unfamiliar surroundings. First explore the immediate vicinity of your home, step by step, with your pet safely on its 6.5-foot (2 m) puppy leash. If your puppy becomes fearful in some situation, don't change course, and don't pick it up and hold it—but don't use force either. Your pet has to be gently taught to overcome its fear. Focus on the "scary object," kneel down, and talk soothingly to the pup. With time, its natural curiosity will win out. A treat offered as a reward will help calm the puppy. Let your pet establish friendly contact with people and other animals. This is critical for its socialization, and it will not undermine subsequent efforts to train it as a protector of home and family (see page 35).

Physical Contact Is Important

Many of the dogs that are brought to me because of problems with their training or their overall behavior are suffering from a common difficulty: Their owners are unable to establish physical contact with them. Intimate partnership between a dog and its master or mistress is a prerequisite for problem-free pet owner-

ship. Starting with physical contact with its littermates, and later with humans, a young dog gradually acquires better control of its movements. In addition, as its "body awareness" develops, its confidence is bolstered and it becomes fully capable of realizing its physical and mental potential. Humans benefit from physical contact with pets as well: Studies have shown that spending a great deal of time in activities with a pet lowers high blood pressure, slows the pulse, and dissipates stress.

Body Contact Exercises

Touch your dog deliberately and consciously, but do not massage it. Working on muscles more intensely might become unpleasant for the dog and do more harm than good. Note the following:

• The exercises should always last for several minutes.

• Pressing gently, make circular motions with your palms and fingertips, so that only the skin over the muscles is moved.

• Start on the dog's abdomen, moving your hands rapidly at first, then more slowly, slowing your breathing at the same time.

• As you work, talk to your pet or hum soothingly, in a deep voice.

• Once the dog is relaxed, let one hand lie still on its body while you continue to work on its entire body systematically, making small circular movements with your other hand.

• If your dog enjoys these few minutes of touching, then you can proceed to more sensitive parts of its body. Carefully work on the skin between its toes and the pads of its feet. Run your index finger and thumb over each ear, moving from the base of the ear to the tip. You can experiment with other areas as well, as your dog gets increasingly used to being touched.

Daily, purposeful physical contact will be beneficial for your dog.

22

Dangers in Your Home and Yard

Source of Danger	Possible Consequences	How to Prevent
Smooth or slippery floors	Broken bones or other injuries	Don't let dog romp around unsupervised.
Sharp or pointed objects	Cuts, puncture wounds	Don't leave dangerous objects lying around.
Indigestible children's toys	Swallowing them can lead to intestinal obstructions.	Don't leave small toys lying around.
Circuit lines, wall sockets	Electric shock (can be fatal)	Unplug cords; block wall sockets with childproof devices.
Chemicals, detergents, cleaning agents, pesticides	Poisoning, acid burns	Store out of the dog's reach; do not use chemical pesticides in your home and yard.
Poisonous house plants and outdoor plants, berries	Poisoning	Do not keep poisonous plants, or put them out of harm's way. Young dogs are particularly at risk. Do not use rat poison, snail bait, or weed killers.
Steep or open stairs	Danger of falling	Use a barrier to deny young dog access (childproof gate).
Balcony	Danger of falling	Attach safety barrier (special gates available in pet stores).
Low window railings	Danger of falling	Open window only from the top; never let dog near an open window unsupervised.
Swimming pool, garden pond	Drowning	Put up safety fence; cover pool with netting; put climbing aids in garden pond; supervise dog when outdoors.
Low fence around yard	Dog may escape.	An escape-proof fence for a German shepherd dog has to be at least 72 inches (180 cm) high, with safeguards at the bottom to keep the dog from digging underneath it to get out.

How German Shepherd Dogs Communicate

Dogs communicate by means of their body language and vocalizations, the roots of which lie deep in their past, in their heritage. Through these means, a dog tells you what is important to it at the moment. To a dog, it is not what *was* or what *will be* that matters—you need to keep this in mind when you are trying to influence your pet. Naturally, young and adult dogs have a better command of "language" than puppies, which first have to practice all the forms of behavior within their pack by playing with their littermates.

Body Language

You will not understand your dog if you pay attention only to isolated signals, such as a wagging tail or laid-back ears. All the body signals given by the dog are meant to be interpreted as a whole; only then will you understand what your pet wants or how it feels at the moment.

Body language is innate. Observance of its rules is possible, however, only if the dog had a chance to practice them repeatedly in its imprinting phases (see page 20). If you fail to offer a dog this opportunity in very early puppyhood, later on you will have a German shepherd dog that cannot adhere to the social rules. That will make it a danger to other—usually smaller—dogs, and it could even kill them with its bite. Conversely, your dog can be seriously injured itself if it runs across a stronger dog and fails to defer to it. It is important for you to learn the meaning of the following body language.

Trying to impress: The dog walks stiff-legged to make itself seem larger. Its eyes are averted, its ears point to the front, and its tail is raised high in the air and waves slightly. Males sometimes turn one side to the other dog or try to impress it by "riding" it. Efforts to intimidate also include marking with urine, followed by digging and scraping.

Threatening to attack: Here the dog lowers its head slightly, but fixes its eyes on its opponent. Its lips are drawn back, and its ears point to the rear. By fully extending its limbs, it tries to look bigger, and it may also bristle its hair. Its tail is extended far over its back. Caution is in order now, since the dog is about to bite.

Important: Dogs have been known to attack without a preliminary warning, immediately after their effort to intimidate. Conversely, a dog also may attack without first trying to intimidate an opponent.

Passive submission: The weaker dog displays passive submission as early as the intimidation phase or, at the latest, during the threat phase, by avoiding eye contact, throwing itself down on its back, pointing its ears to the rear, and simultaneously drawing its lips into a "grin." Its tail is tucked between its legs. On some occasions, however, the dog makes licking motions, whimpers, whines, or cries out. Sometimes it also urinates.

This gesture of lying on its back as a sign of submissiveness causes the stronger dog to leave its opponent alone. Even puppies instinctively use this defensive measure; they lie on their back when faced by adult dogs.

Active submission: The dog's eyes are trustingly and attentively focused on you, and its body and tail are in relaxed positions.

Invitation to play: The dog flattens its forequarters on the ground, looks at you alertly, and raises its hindquarters high in the air, with tail wagging. It alternates between this position and frisky little jumps into the air, moving around you in a circle. It behaves the same way when inviting another dog to play.

Vocalizations

Dogs have a wide range of vocalizations at their command. Even while being nursed, little puppies make "growls" of satisfaction.

Barking: An adult dog barks in a variety of timbres on many different occasions: to warn about strange dogs and animals, to express great joy, or to issue an invitation to play. Sometimes the dog merely "woofs" with closed mouth and slightly inflated cheeks, such as when it is excited by something it cannot identify yet. As a rule, the German shepherd dog has a moderate inclination to bark, and you can encourage or discourage this tendency through training.

Growling: Dogs are able to growl from the second week of life onward. They make this noise later as well, both in play and in earnest, in offensive or defensive situations.

Whimpering: The dog can express submissiveness in this way. It also lends emphasis when the dog is begging for food or asking someone to play. In addition, a dog whimpers when it is in pain. When puppies express their uneasiness or discomfort, they whimper or whine.

Howling: If a dog is left home alone, it often will follow a short period of barking with long, drawn-out howling. A male may howl heartrendingly out of lover's grief. Some dogs howl when they are exposed to high-frequency tones.

Yipping and squealing: Both are signs of great pain or anxiety, particularly in puppies.

"What's in the hole?" "In which one?"

These explorations are really exhausting.

How about another round of "Tug, rip, bite"?

HOW-TO:
Training Your Puppy

Your puppy's training begins the very day it enters its new home. Training procedures for dogs over six months old are described on HOW-TO pages 30 and 31.

Training Rules

• Training is based on the dog's trust in its owner. The trainer has to be consistent and patient.

1) Picking up the puppy the right way: One hand protects the little belly to prevent an umbilical hernia.

• *Roughness and hitting are taboo!* After a successful drill, lavish your pet with praise. You want it to feel that it is being allowed to do something *with* you, not that it *has* to do it.
• Training is not limited to a daily hour of practice or a training course that meets weekly. There you will only receive guidelines that you have to put into effect repeatedly during the rest of the week.
• With a puppy, always squat or crouch when you start an exercise.
• Use body language and facial expressions as you work. The dog will be watching you very closely.
• When giving commands, the most important thing is the tone of your voice, not its volume.
• Always give short commands, using your pet's name; for example: *"Arco! Sit!"* Long sentences will confuse the dog.
• During all the initial exercises, your pet should be hungry, so motivate it with treats. Never play after your dog has been fed, as there is a danger of gastric torsion or stomach upset.
• With all exercises, take a break to play after a few minutes have passed.

Housebreaking
Drawing 1

The first thing the puppy has to learn is to relieve itself outside. Generally, you need to carry it out after every feeding and every nap. Always exit through the same door, and set the dog down at its designated toilet area. When you pick it up, place one hand under its chest and the other beneath its hindquarters (see Drawing 1). Praise and pet the little pup lavishly whenever it relieves itself outdoors. Often the pup will be housebroken within two weeks.

Making its need known: When your puppy has to relieve itself, it will become restless, run to the door, or sit in front of it expec-tantly, walk around sniffing at the floor, and turn around in a circle.

In case of an accident: Punishing your puppy after the fact does no good at all. If the accident happens in your presence, scold the puppy and take it out to its toilet area in the yard. At first, always leave some droppings at that spot to give the puppy the idea. Then it will quickly understand where it is supposed to do its business. Wet spots in your home can be cleaned with a disinfectant or with a solution of vinegar and water.

No or Out
Drawing 2

When the dog hears one of these signals, it should immediately stop whatever it is doing. This is known as putting something under taboo. Utter the commands in a threatening tone of voice. If that doesn't help, firmly take hold of the coat on the puppy's nape. It is all right if

2) Taking the puppy by the scruff is the proper way to scold it.

3) Get your puppy used to the leash early. It should always walk at your left side.

the puppy gives a cry of fear. You can be certain that it will repeatedly test your ability to remain firm. If you give in, you will have lost the battle for good.

Taking something out of its mouth: Place one hand firmly around the dog's muzzle from above. With your fingers, press its lips (flews) firmly against its teeth, saying *"Out!"* in a threatening voice until it lets go of the object. Then praise your pet and reward it with a treat.

Leash Training
Drawing 3

Collar (see Essential Equipment, page 18): Get your puppy accustomed to its collar right away by first having it wear the collar indoors.

Leash (see page 18): The leash is your "telephone line" to the dog, through which you can control it. Hold the leash in your right hand, while the puppy walks at your left. First it has to learn to estimate the area defined by its approximately 6.5-foot (2 m) leash. Before it has a chance to pull the line taut and tug at it, give the leash a short jerk—depending on your pet's degree of stubbornness—and say *"No"* at the same time. Then relax the tension on the leash immediately. With the leash in this slack, but controlled position, you can take the dog for a walk to relieve itself, once it is past puppyhood.

The "Come" Command
Drawing 4

In areas where traffic is not a threat, you can let the puppy run loose, off the leash. Here you need to take advantage of the dog's initial insecurity and show it that it should not go more than about 33 feet (10 m) away from you. If, from that distance, it does not respond to your calling its name or giving the *come* command by immediately running toward you, react either by hiding or by walking off in the opposite direction. Your pup will soon come bounding after you (pack instinct). Praise it or reward it with a little treat.

Important: Never run after the dog. Don't keep announcing your location by calling your pet's name; otherwise, it will always know where you are and will see no reason to come.

4) There is a nice reward for coming and sitting on command.

Sit and Run

To teach your pet these commands, as well as the *down* and *stand* exercises (see page 30), use a sturdy leather or plastic collar and a leather leash about 3 feet (1 m) long.

How to proceed: The puppy, on leash, should stand at your left side. In your right hand, hold the leash and a treat, which you hold over its head so that it has to look upward to see it. Give the *sit* command and call your pet by name. At the same time, gently push down on its hindquarters with your left hand. When it is seated, give it the treat and praise it. After a few seconds, give the *run* command and let it race around and play with you. Practice regularly, until the exercise works with the *sit* command alone.

These two get along great: The German shepherd dog obligingly lets "its" child . . .

Owner and Pet: Living Together

Through consistent training and proper care, the dog will find its subordinate position of rank order within its human/dog pack, and that will allow it to become a well-balanced member of the family. In daily relations, it has to learn over and over that, although it is an integrated family member with the rights appropriate to its species, humans still outrank it. In short—you can allow your pet to do anything and everything, provided it stops immediately on your command.

Following are some small exercises in submission:

• The dog is allowed to lie on the sofa, but has to get down at once—without grumbling—when you direct it to do so.

• It blocks access to a door, but stands up immediately to let you pass through when you so direct it.

If your dog does not comply, always think first about what you might have done wrong.

German Shepherd Dogs and Children

As a family dog, your pet also has to subordinate itself to children or at least to tolerate them. However, the way you raise your children plays an important role in determining whether you and your pet live in harmony.

Smaller children should not be allowed to play with the puppy without supervision. With its sharp little teeth— which will be replaced later—it could give your child a painful nip. Do not leave a small child alone with an adult dog either. If the child accidentally

... *roll it over onto its back.*

A dog is happy when it is playing, but occasionally it needs to have a breather.

sticks a finger in the dog's eye, or gives its tail a hard pull, the dog might defend itself by biting.

Older children have to learn to respect the dog and to treat it properly. It is not a toy, but a living creature that we must take care not to harm. When it is in a resting phase, it does not want to be disturbed. Also show your child the right way to pick up a puppy—not by lifting it up by the forelegs, but by placing one hand under its chest from the front while supporting its hindquarters with the other hand (see drawing, page 26).

Not Everyone Is a Dog Lover

Since our living space is becoming increasingly smaller, keeping a dog in the city will be possible in the future only if owners behave responsibly with their dogs in public and try not to bother or endanger other people. You should set a good example with your German shepherd dog by training it properly and thus making a good impression in public.

• In public areas and parks, always keep the dog on a leash. Do not let your pet play and romp hundreds of yards away from you. Someone who is approaching you and who is afraid of your dog needs to see clearly that you have your pet under control. Also, there is no way you can know how other dogs will behave toward your pet.

• Never leave your pet's droppings in areas frequented by humans—this applies also to large grassy expanses in parks. You can buy scoops and recyclable bags in pet stores for this purpose.

HOW-TO:
Training Your Dog

Start the following exercises when your dog is about six or seven months old (for puppy training and training rules, see page 26; for information on collars and leashes, see page 18).

The Down Exercise
Drawing 1

Start with the dog, on leash, sitting at your left. With your right hand, slowly place a treat on the ground right in front of your pet's nose. When it lowers its nose to the ground as well, move the treat forward a little, giving the *down* command at the same time. The dog will lie down to get to the treat. Give your pet its reward as soon as both the front of its body and its hindquarters are flat on the ground.

1) The gentle approach to teaching the down position: The dog will automatically lie down in order to get to the treat.

2) Use a treat and a taut leash to teach the dog to go from the sit to the standing position.

Pet your dog to keep it in this position for a few seconds. Next, direct it to sit again, then to stand. Keep practicing—never more than three times in a row, however—until the dog lies down in response to the *down* command alone. Gradually extend the time it maintains that position to one minute.

Down and Stay
Drawing 4

When the dog can be counted on to perform the *down* command, hold up one hand, palm toward the dog and arm outstretched, as if trying to stop traffic. Then slowly take one or two steps backward, while giving the *stay* command. As you do so, praise the dog in a soft voice and tell it to stay lying down.

Important: If the dog wants to come to you, quickly say *"No"* in a threatening voice. If that

doesn't help, repeat *"No"* with indignation, return the dog to the *down* position, and start the exercise over again.

Start with a few seconds, and gradually extend the dog's waiting time (up to two minutes) and your distance from the dog. Do not give the *run* signal until you have gone back to your dog, which should be still in the *down* position. Repeat this exercise a few times. Remember that during your first efforts, you should never call your dog to come to you from its *down* position or you will not be able to rely on it to maintain that *down* position in the future.

Sit and Stay

If the dog will stay in the *down* position for up to two minutes, you can also teach it the *sit and stay* command. Since it has already mastered the *sit* (see page 27), proceed exactly as with the *down and stay* exercise, above.

The Stand Exercise
Drawing 2

Have your pet, now seven to eight months old, sit—on leash—at your left side. Hold the leash and a treat in your right hand. As you move the treat out in front of you, away from the dog's nose, the leash will grow taut. Encourage your pet to get to its feet by simultaneously saying *"Stand."*

Once the dog is on its feet, keep it in this position for several seconds by gently placing your left hand on the inside of its left thigh and giving it its treat, while saying a few soothing words.

3) With the leash slack, the dog heels, keeping even with your left foot.

Then release it again with the *run* command. Soon it will move from the *sit* position to the *stand* position on the *stand* command alone.

Stand and stay: Once the dog has mastered the *stand* exercise, you can teach it the *stand and stay* exercise.

The Heel Exercise
Drawing 3

By now the puppy has learned not to tug at the 6.5-foot (2 m) long leash. At the age of six to seven months it is ready to practice walking with the leash slack, keeping its right shoulder even with your left foot, in response to the *heel* command.

Collar and leash: Use a link collar, set so as not to pull, and a leash about 3 feet (1 m) long, sturdy enough to be jerked without breaking.

How to proceed: Start with the dog sitting at your left side.

Holding the leash in your right hand, shorten it so that it hangs barely slack. Say *"Heel"* and walk forward, starting off with your left foot.

If the dog lags behind, encourage it to come along. If it forges ahead, correct it with a short, vigorous jerk on the leash with your left hand, at lightning speed (see Leash Training, page 27). At the same time, stand still, then move forward only a step at a time, once the dog is back in the right place.

Important: After the jerk, you should immediately let the leash hang slack again. If you maintain the tension or even pull the dog back, it will intensify its efforts to move forward.

Incorporating changes in pace: At first, don't walk too fast. Increase your tempo only when the dog is moving correctly. If it slows down, don't drag it along behind you; instead, use body language and a faster pace to encourage it to catch up. Always go from your normal tempo to a faster or slower pace.

Practicing changes of direction: To keep your dog alert, don't walk in a straight line all the time. If the dog tries to change course, make a sudden about turn to the right or a precise right turn with a short jerk on the leash. At the same time, employ body language; for example, pat the inside of your pet's left thigh with your left hand or bend your knees slightly when making the turns.

Heeling Off Leash
Do not try heeling without the leash until your dog can execute certain exercises—straight ahead, right turn, left turn, about turn, normal pace, slow pace, and run—with the leash slack and while staying close to your left leg, without needing any leash corrections.

Important: Never let the dog run loose near a heavily traveled street. Being an animal, it will react instinctively and unpredictably, despite the best training. If accidents occur, you are responsible.

4) The outstretched hand gives a message to the dog: "Stay in your place."

Activities and Advanced Training Programs

The German shepherd dog, with its multitude of talents and abilities, absolutely *must* have meaningful, appropriate activities and advanced training. The fact is that the most common cause of dangerous behavioral disturbances—besides inappropriate, inconsistent training—is these agile dogs' "joblessness."

Play Will Keep Your Pet Fit

With its intelligence and desire to work, this dog enjoys learning as it plays, and carrying out tasks. Playing together not only will keep your pet physically and mentally fit, but also will contribute substantially to a good relationship between you and your dog. Today, you have a great many opportunities for engaging in recreational sports with your dog (see HOW-TO: Physical Fitness Program, pages 34 and 35). In addition, you can join a good dog sports club in your neighborhood. Information is available from the German Shepherd Club of America (see Useful Addresses, page 62).

Important: Before beginning any athletic activity, have a veterinarian examine your pet to determine whether the activity is a suitable one. Getting a sick dog involved in sports is cruel to the animal.

How to Find a Good Dog Club

Do not choose a club until you have visited its training center several times to observe the classes held there. The following questions will help you assess the club:
• Does the club offer a multifaceted program?
• Are you and your pet given a friendly reception?
• Is your dog being evaluated primarily in terms of its suitability for breeding?
• Do the members treat their own dogs with kindness?
• Do the classes cover theory as well as practice?
• Are spiked collars, electrical devices, or strong-arm methods used during the training sessions?

Guard Dog Training

Guard dog training is an activity that can be beneficial to both owner and dog. Although clubs often sponsor guard dog training seminars, dogs are usually trained and evaluated individually, not in classes. Training your German shepherd dog for home or family protection makes great demands upon the dog, and even greater demands on you as the owner or trainer. Before embarking on a guard dog training program, you should carefully consider the age and personality of the dog to be trained. Aggressive dogs must be trained with great care to avoid attacking without provocation. Dogs must be totally obedient before training is begun, and every step of attack training should be under the direction of an experienced guard dog trainer.

Tired after playing boisterously, this puppy is taking a break; very soon it will start a new game.

Enthusiastically, this 15-week-old puppy sprints through the agility tunnel in its obstacle course.

The Right Club Trainer

Appropriate programs of basic and advanced training for dogs stand or fall with the quality of the club's trainers. Since no formal qualifications are required for this honorary function, you need to judge for yourself, using the following criteria.

A good trainer will:
• present the club to you in its entirety, as well as tell you about the various training objectives and facilities for sports;
• engage in a lengthy conversation to gather information about your dog's care and living conditions, special characteristics, and problems, as well as your purpose in training your pet;
• not only teach you the mechanical procedures, but explain to you why his or her way of handling the dog's practical training is appropriate.

Sports Take Time

At least during the training phase, you will have little time for other leisure activities. With that in mind, I suggest the following:
• Take your dog to the club for athletic activities twice a week.
• At least one or two hours a day, you and your dog must practice what you have learned from the club trainer.
• Keep in mind that trials or competitions—whatever the sport—are often held on weekends.

HOW-TO:
Physical Fitness Programs

Walking

A 30-minute walk three times a day—in addition to sports—is the minimum required by a healthy dog. Racing around in your yard is no substitute for contact with the outside world. The dog needs to pick up "olfactory" impressions and meet other members of its species.

1) The dog needs to be able to set the pace, and it has to be healthy and well trained.

Bicycling
Drawing 1

Do not take the dog along as a companion on a bike ride until its physical development is complete (about one year old). The dog—on leash at first—should run at the right side of the bike. Start with ten minutes of biking and gradually increase that time. Long trips of more than one hour could harm the dog, because it cannot control the pace itself, in accordance with its own capacity. If the dog obeys all your commands and if it has learned to run correctly beside the bicycle, you can leave the leash off in rural areas, if you like, but never within city limits.

Tracking Work
Drawing 4

Tracking, in the form of a game, can be integrated into your walk. There is one requirement: A second person—someone known to the dog—has to accompany you. While your pet stays behind with your companion, you walk away and hide behind a tree. You can mark your path every few yards with treats. When your companion gives the *go find* command, the dog will begin to track you. When it finds you, shower it with praise.

Tournament Sports (Combined Sports)

This kind of sport usually takes the form of a four-discipline competition:

1. Obedience exercises
2. Hurdle race
3. Slalom (weave-pole) race
4. Obstacle course

With disciplines 2 and 4, the emphasis is on absence of errors and speed. The handler is always at the side of the dog.

Agility
Drawings 2 and 3

Agility, a type of dog sport that came to this country from England, provides fitness training for both dog and owner.

Obstacle course: An obstacle course, which varies in design from event to event, has to be negotiated by the dog and directed by its handler, without errors and as speedily as possible. In contrast to tournament sports, where the handler is always at the dog's side, here the dog is supposed to be controlled at certain distances as well.

Flyball

In this sport, which originated in the United States, two teams, each with four dogs, start at the same time. Each dog, at its handler's command, has to clear four

2) Courage and physical agility are required for negotiating this cross-over. Teach your dog slowly, on leash.

34

relatively small hurdles, press down the pedal of a ball machine, catch the ball tossed out by the machine, and carry it back over the four hurdles and across the finish line. If it has crossed the line without making a mistake, the next dog in the group can start the course. The team that is the first to have all four dogs cross the finish line without any mistakes is the winner.

Competitive Sports: Security Dog Exam

It is interesting to note that in some countries, for example Germany, for a German shepherd dog to receive approval to breed, one of the requirements is passing the Security Dog Exam, Level I. This covers three areas:

1. *Subordination* (100 points): Obedience and agility exercises are scored strictly according to a point system, in terms of accuracy and willingness.

2. *Tracking* (100 points): In a meadow or a field, an assistant lays a scent trail, changing direction several times and placing several small objects on the ground, depending on the achievement level being tested. After a certain waiting period, the dog, on a 33-foot (10 m) leash, has to follow the trail with its nose to the ground, and find the objects placed there. In evaluating mistakes, the judge takes into account the dog's precision of execution.

3. *Security work* (100 points): The dog has to find, bring to bay, and bark at a hidden person, resist an attack upon itself or its handler, catch a fleeing person

and fight off his or her attacker; this is clearly designed as a test of courage. Points are deducted for mistakes, such as biting someone being held at bay.

What critics say: Again and again, critics claim that training dogs for security work makes them inclined to attack humans. It is important to note:

• A good security training assistant uses only the family dog's innate desire to *pursue* quarry in teaching it to *capture* quarry, not—as in training for police work—its instinct to offer resistance, which would make it into a true police dog.

• Unqualified security training assistants can unconsciously promote the dog's instinct to resist by improper instruction. Some trainers do this consciously as well—even without the dog owner's knowledge—in order to boost the training status of the dogs in their club.

3) With a treat as an incentive, speed and agility are quickly learned (here, weave poles in an agility course).

Important: Before you decide to have your dog trained to protect your home and family, you need to observe some training sessions and decide whether you and your pet are equal to these demands. For the dog, nothing is worse than an interrupted training course.

4) Using its nose to find a hidden object: This game can be incorporated into every walk.

Feeding and Nutrition

How Wolves Subsist

Like its ancestor, the wolf, the dog is also a meat-eating or carnivorous animal. In the strict sense, however, the term "meat-eater" is not entirely accurate, since the wolf does not eat the flesh of its prey exclusively.

The wolf eats plant-eaters (herbivores) that it has hunted and killed or found dead. When it kills a relatively large prey, it first uses its teeth to tear open the other animal's abdominal wall, and consumes the stomach contents, along with the stomach and entrails, which are filled with predigested plant matter. Thus, the wolf's organism is supplied not only with protein, found in the flesh of its prey, but also with carbohydrates and minerals that are present in its victim's blood, stomach contents, bones, and hair. In varying amounts, the wolf also eats fruits, grasses, roots, leaves, other animals' excrement, and other wastes.

If one assumes that the natural diet of the domestic dog evolved from that of the wolf, it becomes clear that in the dog's case, what matters most is a well-balanced mix of foodstuffs that contain all the vital nutrients.

Puppies need a well-balanced diet that includes vitamins and minerals.

Commercial Dog Food

Most commercial dog foods are precisely formulated to meet the dog's needs. They contain all the substances that are important in a healthy diet for a dog. A large number of food varieties—in the form of moist (or canned), semimoist, and dry foods—are commercially available.

Wet or canned dog food has a moisture rating of 75 to 85 percent. Two kinds are available:
- Dog food that is 100 percent meat (chicken, tuna, muscle meats, tripe, liver, and lung, for example).
- Dog food that is supplemented with carbohydrates in the form of cereals (rice, barley, oats, wheat, or corn)

My tip: Always mix all-meat dog food with vegetable or cereal flakes (packaged product), to avoid an unbalanced diet (lack of carbohydrates). The mixing ratio is: ⅔ canned dog food and ⅓ flakes.

Semimoist and dry dog foods are also nutritionally complete, but they contain less water (10 to 30 percent) than canned foods and thus are more concentrated and higher in energy. There is no need to add cereal flakes to them. If you feed your pet dry food exclusively, it will need sufficient fresh water to drink, so that it can get enough liquid intake.

My tip: From my practical experience, I know that some dogs do not always tolerate an exclusive diet of canned food and, in some cases, they may even refuse to eat it. For this reason, I always feed my dogs all-natural, untreated products, very few of which are canned.

Basic Elements in the Diet

A dog's daily diet has to contain the following ingredients in adequate amounts:

Protein is found in meat, fish, and dairy products. The following are suitable for feeding your pet: beef, horse

This German shepherd dog loves "its" cat. While Kitty eats, the dog even washes its fur.

meat, venison, lamb, poultry (without bones!), and fish.

Depending on the dog's age, its diet should consist of 25 to 60 percent meat. I feed my dogs raw meat, since I use only meat that has been officially inspected. If your dog does not tolerate raw meat, you can cook it before giving it to your pet.

Caution: Raw pork may contain the virus that causes Aujeszky's disease, which is fatal in dogs. Salmonella can be transmitted through raw poultry. All pathogens are destroyed by cooking.

Fats are present in adequate amounts in mixed meats. The fat content should not exceed 5 percent. In addition, 1 tablespoon of cold-pressed vegetable oil (wheat germ oil) should be added to the daily food ration. In winter, also add 1 tablespoon of cod-liver oil.

Carbohydrates in the form of boiled unpolished (brown) rice or whole oat flakes should not exceed 40 percent of the total food amount. Feed your pet boiled noodles or mashed potatoes only as an exception.

To preserve and care for its teeth, your German shepherd dog needs something hard to bite. The best things to give it are dried rawhide "bones" or strips of rawhide. These will prevent tartar buildup.

Minerals, such as calcium, phosphorus, and sodium, as well as a large number of other mineral substances that influence body processes (copper, iodine, sulfur, and fluorine and magnesium compounds), are essential ingredients of your pet's diet. It is best to use a commercially available mineral preparation, following the package directions (available from veterinarians and in pet stores).

Note: If you use ready-to-serve flakes or dry dog food that contains added vitamins, there is no need to use mineral supplements as well.

Vitamins are present in fruits, vegetables (including garlic and onions), cod-liver oil, and brewers' yeast. Finely chopped young dandelion leaves, parsley, and other potherbs, as well as proper dosages of medicinal herbs, make a very healthful supplement. Fruits and herbs, however, should not account for more than two heaping tablespoons of a dog's daily amount of food.

Vegetables and fruits should be puréed in a blender, so they will not be difficult for the dog to digest.

Note: Don't give your pet beans or spicy, peppery types of vegetables.

Roughage cannot be broken down by the dog's gastric acid, but in small quantities it aids the action of the intestines and thus promotes healthy digestion. Roughage is found in whole-grain flakes, rice, and a number of raw vegetables, such as carrots and kohlrabi (but be sure to purée the vegetables, as mentioned above).

Bones are not a suitable food for dogs (there is a danger of constipation), but they can be useful in your pet's dental care program, as they help prevent tartar from forming on the teeth. Twice a week, offer your dog a fairly large beef bone (a joint head or the like).

Caution: Do not give your dog poultry or venison bones, since these long, cylindrical bones will splinter and injure its intestines.

For chewing, the following are the best choices for your German shepherd dog: rawhide strips and "bones," and similar nylon and rubber articles. Besides providing some benefit in tartar removal (not to replace regular dental care!), these items also give a teething puppy or a bored adult a suitable alternative to the furniture or your clothing. Hard, dry whole-grain bread is also an excellent supplementary food.

Note: Seasoned leftovers from your own table or from restaurants, leftover sausages, and sweets are harmful to your pet's health.

Food Preparation, Feeding "Techniques," and Food Amounts

Preparation: The prepared food should be served at room temperature, and should not be overly soupy in consistency.

Feeding "techniques": Let your pet watch while you prepare its meal; that will spur its appetite. Do not disturb the dog while it is eating. Ideally, it will empty its bowl quickly. If it stops eating and goes away from the food bowl, remove the bowl at once, along with any uneaten food. At the next meal, give your pet less food.

If your pet licks the bowl clean as a sign that it got too little to eat, do not increase the serving at the next meal. Never let your dog have a second helping; otherwise, in the future it will decide itself how much it is going to eat. Stand near your dog while it eats. After it finishes, remove the bowl immediately, wash it in warm water, and put it away.

My tip: Don't spoil your dog with little between-meal treats, such as dog biscuits. Little tidbits given as rewards should be available only when you are working with your pet.

Note: Do not play or work with the dog for two to three hours after it has eaten a large meal, in order to prevent gastric torsion, see page 52).

Amounts of food: Dogs differ in terms of their capacity to respond to proper care and feeding. The amount of food depends on the demands you make on your dog. You yourself have to learn over time how much food your pet requires. For some guidelines, see Feeding Plan, below.

Where and When to Feed

Where: The food and water utensils should always be placed in the same spot.

When: Give young dogs three to four meals a day. Even an adult dog needs to be fed twice a day; it is better for its health. With dogs over eight years old, divide the ration into three meals a day. Always feed your pet at the same times of day.

Drinking Water Is Crucial

Fresh water has to be available to your pet at all times. Be aware, however, that milk can cause diarrhea if consumed within a four-hour period before or after a meal that includes meat.

Feeding Plan

The following combinations and amounts of food have worked extremely well with my dogs:

From the second month of life on, divided into three to four meals: 12 to 14 ounces (350–400 g) of lean beef (muscle meat), mixed with wheat flakes or boiled rice: (60 percent meat and 40 percent flakes or rice).

Also spread out over the daily ration: 1 tablespoon wheat-germ oil, 1 tea-

It is all right to use a treat as a reward for obeying a command.

spoon cod-liver oil, mineral supplement as directed on the package, minced or grated vegetables and herbs (a total of 1 heaping tablespoon per day), one half clove of garlic.

Twice a week, one cooked egg yolk (without the white). Two to three times a week: soft veal bones, which you can let the puppy's little teeth work on under your supervision.

Note: Bone meal contains calcium in extremely pure form. Since young dogs' feces often is pasty, add about ½ teaspoon bone meal to the food until the stool is firm.

From the fourth month on, divided into three meals: 12 ounces (350 g) of beef, mixed with flakes or boiled rice

Vitality is a sign of good health. A powerful sprint propels this dog through the water.

(60 percent meat and 40 percent wheat flakes or rice), as well as supplements, as described above for the second month on. Now you can let your pet chew on rawhide between meals to help it cut its new teeth.

From the sixth month on, divided into two meals: 12 to 21 ounces (350–600 g) of beef, depending on feeding conditions, flakes or boiled rice (60 percent meat, 40 percent wheat flakes or rice), as well as supplements, as described above for the second month on.

If the dog's coat is not healthy-looking, add 1 teaspoon brewer's yeast to its food daily.

From the twelfth month on, divided into two meals: 14 to 17.5 ounces (400–500 g) of mixed beef (meat from various parts of the cow's body, including cartilage), flakes or boiled rice (60 percent meat, 40 percent flakes or rice). Add bone meal, if stool consistency requires, as well as the following supplements: 1 tablespoon wheat-germ oil; from October to March, also 1 teaspoon cod-liver oil, 1 tablespoon brewer's yeast (powdered), and finely chopped or grated vegetables and herbs.

Two to three times a week, add 1 cooked egg yolk (without white) and fist-sized veal bones after the main meal. On these days, do not add bone meal.

Note: If necessary, give the dog only a half-ration of food one day a week, to keep it trim and in shape

Suggestions for Breakfast

The following morning snack is appropriate from the sixth month of life on, to give energy to a dog that engages in sports or performs work.

A German shepherd dog would rather bathe itself in a lake than be shampooed in your tub.

Depending on the dog's age, mix 1.7 to 3.5 ounces (50–100 g) of farmer cheese, milk, and flakes to a soupy consistency; add one egg yolk and 1 level teaspoon honey.

Note: Wait about five hours before serving your pet a meal containing meat to avoid the possibility of diarrhea. Even with the breakfast, there is no need to reduce your pet's daily ration. If the dog looks overweight, you can cut down on the meat rations.

A Fat Dog—What Do I Do Now?

Excess weight involves a great many health risk factors for a dog and can substantially shorten its life. Shortness of breath, heart and circulatory problems, digestive problems, and excessive stress on tendons and joints are only a few examples.

The "figure" test: If you can no longer feel the dog's ribs at mid-chest level behind its shoulder blades, and it no longer has a discernible "waistline," your pet is too fat. Careful reduction of the excess weight is called for.

Healthy weight loss: First and foremost, have a veterinarian confirm that the dog is overweight; he or she might detect possible organic causes for the extra pounds. Depending on the causes of the excess weight, the veterinarian will prescribe a weight-loss diet for the dog. Today, there are excellent diet foods commercially available (from veterinarians or in pet stores) to help you control your dog's weight.

Grooming and Health Check

Regular grooming of a dog is an important hygienic measure, a necessary procedure whenever humans and animals live together. In addition, well-groomed dogs are less disease-prone, and giving your animal attention in this way strengthens the bond between you and your dog.

Daily coat care keeps your German shepherd dog healthy as well as beautiful. Spending time with your pet while grooming it deepens the bond between you and the dog.

Start Grooming in Puppyhood

It is best to get your pet used to grooming procedures, such as taking care of its coat, inspecting its teeth, and cleaning its ears, while it is still a puppy, even though these procedures are performed on a much smaller scale than in the case of a full-grown dog.

By starting early, your pet will learn what it is like to be lifted onto a table, to keep quiet, to stand still, and to lie down, and as an adult dog it will be more apt to enjoy the grooming process than to submit to it reluctantly.

Note: On HOW-TO pages 46 and 47, you will find step-by-step descriptions of the individual procedures.

Health Check from A to Z

During grooming, which involves close contact with the dog, you also need to be on the lookout for any symptoms of disease. Changes in behavior are the first noticeable signs of a possible illness. The animal will appear sad, listless, surly, or ill-tempered. It moves around from one place to another, is restless, runs aimlessly to and fro, whimpers, groans, cries out when touched, howls, or is fearful or confused. It seems indifferent to its surroundings, has a vacant stare, moves slowly and haltingly, or sleeps a great deal.

During the grooming process you may notice physical symptoms of illness as well. Pay attention to the following:

Bad breath: Diseased teeth or a stomach ailment may be the cause. Consult the veterinarian.

Body build: Substantial weight loss or gain may be a symptom of disease.

Body temperature: The normal temperature of a dog is between 100 and 102.5°F (37.5–38°C) (see Taking the Dog's Temperature, page 50).

Coat: Dull, dry hair with a reddish tinge, as well as brittle hair, often are signs of malnutrition. However, it is normal for the coat to lose its gloss before new hair growth occurs in spring and fall.

Ears: If the dog repeatedly tilts its head to one side, shakes it frequently, and keeps scratching at its ear, it probably has dirt in its inner ear or an ear infection due to ear mites. Their presence can cause a dark, dirty, waxy material to adhere to the inner skin of the ears. If you suspect ear mites, seek professional help to combat these pests, which are usually transmitted through contract with infected animals.

Eyes: They should be clear. Reddened eyes and a discharge are indications of conjunctivitis; clouded eyes point to some other disease. See a veterinarian.

Feet: If the pads are cracked, rubbing them with petroleum jelly will help. Overly long nails have to be clipped (see page 47). When grooming this area, also check for injuries on your pet's feet and foreign bodies between its toes.

Gums: The gums should be rose-pink in color; reddened gums are a sign of inflammation.

Lips, flews (pendulous corners of upper lip): They should be firm and "closed," not drooping; however, there are some German shepherd dogs whose flews naturally droop slightly. Where that occurs, the lips, not infrequently, are affected by chapping or lip eczema, where hard crusts form at the corners of the mouth, and they have to be treated by a veterinarian. Regularly cleaning the flews and rubbing petroleum jelly into them will prevent such problems.

Lymph glands: The lymph glands are palpable between the hinge of the jaw (temporomandibular joint) and the ear. If they are swollen, that points to the presence of an infection. See the veterinarian.

Mucous membranes: Unusually pale or otherwise altered coloration of the mucous membranes—the conjunctiva and the mucous membrane inside the mouth, for example—is a symptom of disease.

Pulse rate: The dog's pulse beats 60 to 80 times a minute. The rate can rise because of anxiety, fear, or joy, and after physical exertion. Take your pet's pulse on the inside of its thigh. At rest, the dog takes 12 to 24 breaths per minute.

Sex organs: A discharge when a female is not in heat may be an indication of metritis (inflammation of the uterus). In males, yellowish drops often collect on the foreskin of the penis. In these cases, consult a veterinarian.

Skin: Symptoms of disease include discoloration of the skin on the inner thighs and the abdomen; dry, hard, hot, or cold skin; foul-smelling perspiration; pale or doughy swellings of the skin that are insensitive to pain.

Dandruff, eczema, reddish areas, and frequent scratching in connection with dry, brittle hair may be induced by improper nutrition. Sebaceous cysts are caused when a hair follicle is injured or crushed; it then fills with a creamy substance and resembles a large blackhead. Don't squeeze out the matter inside! See the veterinarian.

Stool: The dog's stool should be firm, compact, not overly hard, and sausage-shaped. With protracted diarrhea or diarrhea accompanied by blood in the stool, vomiting, or fever, see the veterinarian. For short bouts of diarrhea that are not accompanied by blood or fever, have your pet fast for a day.

Find out whether improper feeding has caused the diarrhea. For constipation that lasts more than one day, see the veterinarian; you may have given the dog too many bones. From time to time, check your pet's stool to see whether any worms (see page 48) have been passed.

Teeth: Tartar (dental calculus), a yellowish deposit on the teeth, has to be removed by the veterinarian. To prevent tartar, give your pet predominantly solid foods to chew, as well as

The German shepherd dog loves to run. For this reason you need to check the areas between the pads of its feet on a regular basis.

This German shepherd dog proudly allows the finishing grooming touches to be applied.

veterinarian-approved chew toys and dental exercisers, designed to help remove tartar and plaque (see Dental Care, page 46).

Urine: The dog's urine should be released in a stream, not in drops; it has a slightly garlicky smell. It should be pale yellow to dark yellow in color.

Important: If you think your pet may be ill, see the veterinarian without delay!

Should I Bathe My Dog?

The short hair of the German shepherd dog is very easy to take care of, and it does not get dirty easily; a daily brushing, however, is advisable. The double coat consists of the so-called top, or outer, coat and the undercoat. The hairs of the former lie like roof shingles on the dog's skin and protect the undercoat against dampness.

As a rule, German shepherd dogs enjoy the water. When the weather is hot, they love to play with the water hose and to take a little shower in the yard. Therefore, bathing your pet to get it clean—unless it is extremely dirty or smelly—is necessary only during spring and fall, when its new coat is growing in.

How to do it: Place the dog on a nonskid surface in the bathtub. Using a moisturizing shampoo for dogs, put some in a small container and dilute it with lukewarm water. Spray the dog thoroughly with lukewarm water, then rub the shampoo into its coat, keeping one hand over its eyes to shield them. Rinse the dog thoroughly again. If necessary, repeat the process. Finally, dry the dog well, but do not use a blow dryer, which would make its skin too dry.

In summer, after you bathe your pet, go for a walk with the dog on leash, until its coat is dry.

In winter, put the dog into a warm, draft-free room to dry. Don't put it into its kennel outdoors while its coat is still damp, as it could become chilled.

Removing Parasites

Fleas and ticks are among the most common parasites that infest dogs.

Fleas can be picked up anywhere by your pet. They are especially active during the warm months of the year. If your dog scratches itself frequently, it may have fleas. Examine its coat thoroughly; flea excrement is visible as tiny, dark dots on the skin. Fleas also can be transmitted to humans.

The veterinarian or a pet store can supply you with a special shampoo for bathing your dog, or with a special powder and an anti-flea spray. You need to disinfect the place where the dog sleeps and the floor at the same time, because these little pests also are present in the dog's surroundings. It is important to repeat the treatment after about one week, since new fleas can hatch from eggs that have not been killed, and reinfest your pet.

Note: Tick and flea collars have only limited suitability, because they give off insecticides with which the dog will be in close physical contact.

Ticks: They are especially common in warm, damp months. Check your pet's skin for ticks every time you return from a walk in the woods, and every time your dog has been in bushes or underbrush.

It is best to remove ticks with ordinary tweezers or with special tick tweezers (available in pet stores).

Use the tweezers to grab the tick as close to the dog's skin as possible, pulling *very* slowly on the tick's head and mouth. Be certain to get all of the tick out of your dog's skin, and then put alcohol or another antiseptic on the bite.

Not only are ticks a nuisance, they also carry a life-threatening disease: *Borelliosis* or *Lyme disease.*

Lyme disease, first identified in Lyme, Connecticut, is spread primarily by the deer tick, a tiny bloodsucker credited with carrying an illness that can do your dog—and you—great physical harm! Borelliosis can affect your dog in several ways, but usually swelling and tenderness around the joints are present. If you find a tick on your dog, or suspect that the dog has been bitten by a tick, contact your veterinarian immediately.

If you have been bitten by a tick or see the telltale tick bite surrounded by a characteristic red ring, consult your physician or county health department. In both cases—yours and the dog's—timely diagnosis and treatment are essential!

My tip: Add half a teaspoon of garlic to your pet's daily rations. Generally, it will act as a tick preventive.

A puppy has to learn how to clean itself.

HOW-TO:
Grooming

Regular grooming is important not only to keep your dog looking good, but to keep it healthy as well. Essential procedures involved in grooming a dog are described below.

Grooming Utensils
Drawing 1

You need appropriate "tools" for grooming. These include a wide-toothed comb, a flea comb, a hard-bristled brush, a toothbrush, nail clippers, a nail file, and tick tweezers.

Combing and Brushing
Drawing 2

To keep your German shepherd dog's coat glossy, you need to comb and brush it daily.

How to do it: Position the dog with the front of its body slightly elevated, so that its skin will be taut (for example, put its front paws on the lowest stair of your staircase). With a hard-bristled brush, brush the hair with long strokes, against the lie. Next, brush the hair smooth again, with the lie. Finally, use a comb to remove loose hairs. Comb the tail thoroughly with a wide-toothed comb.

Note: During shedding season, use a special currying brush and a comb to remove loose undercoat hairs.

Eye Care

You should check your dog's eyes on a daily basis. After it wakes up, use a damp tissue to remove any secretions that have accumulated in the corners of its eyes. You can soften encrusted matter with water (*not* boric acid solution) in advance. Check to see whether the conjunctiva is reddened or inflamed (see page 43).

2) First brush the hair against the direction of growth; then brush it smooth again.

Ear Care
Drawing 3

If your pet's ears are dirty, put a few drops of ear cleanser (available from your veterinarian) into each ear. Next, carefully knead the outside of the ear at its base. After the dog shakes itself, clean the external part of the ear with a piece of cotton wrapped around your little finger. Do *not* use a cotton swab; it is all too easy to push it too deeply into the auditory canal and injure the eardrum.

Note: If the dog cries out in pain when you knead its ear from the outside, an inflammation is present. It is essential to take the dog to the veterinarian at once.

Dental Care
Drawing 4

The teeth of your German shepherd dog have to be checked regularly. Some dogs have a tendency to tartar buildup, which can result in

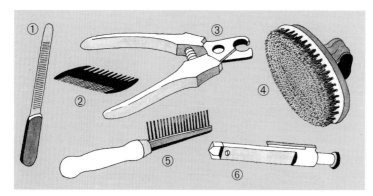

1) The major grooming utensils at a glance: (1) nail file, (2) flea comb, (3) nail clippers, (4) coat brush with hard bristles, (5) wide-toothed comb, (6) tick tweezers.

gingivitis and even in tooth loss. Tartar is visible as a brownish coating at the base of the tooth.

Regularly brushing your pet's teeth with a hard-bristled toothbrush (special toothpaste is available from the veterinarian or in a pet store; do *not* use toothpaste meant for humans) can prevent tartar. As an alternative, give the dog dried rawhide, whole-grain bread, or similar things to chew.

From time to time, rub the dog's teeth with a slice of lemon.

Note: Tartar has to be removed by the veterinarian. If you discover that your pet has a loose or broken tooth, if the dog drools excessively, or if it has bad breath, consult the veterinarian. It may be that some teeth are suppurating and will have to be pulled.

Foot Care

Rub petroleum jelly into cracked, dry feet.

After a walk, check your pet's feet and remove any asphalt, small stones, or other foreign objects adhering to them, or stuck between the pads.

In winter, use a good baby salve, cod-liver oil salve, or any salve with a glycerine base on your dog's feet before taking a walk, to protect them against thawing salt. When you come home from walks, wash the dirt and salt off the paws with some warm water in a shallow plastic tub. Then dry the feet well and apply some petroleum jelly to the pads to keep them soft.

Nail Care

Normally the nails are worn down when the dog moves over a hard surface; however, especially with old dogs that move around less, the nails may grow too long and become a hindrance. They need a special "pedicure"— the nails have to be trimmed.

Let the veterinarian show you how to clip your dog's nails. The problem is that blood vessels and nerve endings extend into the nails, and they can be injured when you trim the nail.

Overly sharp nails in a puppy can be smoothed and rounded with a nail file.

Cleaning the Skin of the Nose

After your dog has been doing "excavation work," wash off the dirt on the nose with a dampened sponge and lubricate the skin of the nose with petroleum jelly.

Elbow Care

Over time, leathery, often cracked areas develop on the elbows, as the dog leans on these areas for support when it lies down. You need to rub these spots regularly with petroleum jelly or cod-liver ointment.

Anal Care

If the anal glands do not empty themselves when the dog has a bowel movement, inflammation will result. Have the veterinarian show you where these very important "scent glands" are located.

Sticky areas (resulting from diarrhea, for example) need to be cleaned with a dampened sponge. Then lubricate the anal area with marigold (calendula) ointment.

Note: If a dog keeps "scooting" around on its bottom, this may be an indication of worms or of inflamed anal glands. In either case, you must take your pet to the veterinarian.

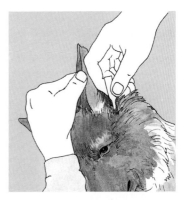

3) To clean the auditory canals, put in drops of cleaning solution, at room temperature.

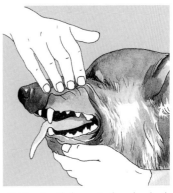

4) The teeth have to be checked regularly for tartar or injuries.

Preventive Care and Diseases

Even with proper care, your German shepherd dog may become sick. If you notice changes in your pet, don't postpone the trip to the veterinarian. The earlier a disease is detected and treated, the better the chances for a cure.

Vaccination Gives Immunity

There are effective immunizations against rabies, distemper, hepatitis, canine parvovirus, and leptospirosis. To ensure complete immunity, the dog has to be vaccinated according to a certain schedule. The puppy gets its first shots, the so-called basic series, before it leaves the breeder. These inoculations and the dates for subsequent booster shots are recorded in the vaccination certificate (see page 16). A few days after you bring the puppy home, take it to the veterinarian to discuss the appointments for the next shots.

Important: Be sure to have the dog wormed before being vaccinated.

Worming

Roundworms and *tapeworms* are the most common intestinal parasites. They can attack the dog at any stage of life and weaken its resistance. A puppy is first wormed at the age of two weeks, then at four, six, and eight weeks of age. Then the first vaccination follows. At 12 weeks, the dog is wormed again; then it is given the second vaccination. Finally, it is wormed again at the age of six months and once more at nine months.

This long-haired male has an alert, proud appearance. The black spot on its tongue does not diminish its noble look.

A full-grown dog should be given a worm treatment twice a year. If the dog is often infested with fleas, however, more frequent worming may be necessary, since the most common tapeworm in dogs is carried by fleas.

Note: Ask the veterinarian for advice before you are purchase a worm remedy.

My tip: Worm adult dogs only when their stool shows signs of a worm infestation; frequent worming can damage the intestinal cells.

Detecting Signs of Illness

In the chapter "Grooming and Health Check" (beginning on page 42), I listed behavioral changes that are indicators of disease. If the following symptoms appear, take your pet to the veterinarian without delay:
• The dog refuses to eat or eats to excess.
• It refuses to drink or drinks too much.
• It has protracted diarrhea or constipation.
• It vomits frequently.
• It has difficulty breathing and pants, even at rest.
• It sways, staggers, or loses consciousness.
• It suffers from severe itching and bites at its feet until they have open sores.
• Its pulse is too high or too low at rest (see page 43).
• The dog has trouble getting to its feet, or it whines or cries out when climbing stairs.

Repeated vaccinations are essential to a dog's health—but who in this photo is suffering the most?

- Blood is present in its urine or stool.
- It has fever (see page 42).

  Note: Depending on the disease, the symptoms listed above may appear in combination.

Mental Disturbances

The "psyche" of your German shepherd dog is just as vulnerable as that of a human. Sudden neglect, experiences involving shock (for example, resulting from an accident or a beating), separa- tion from its family, and even a tempo- rary stay in a boarding kennel during your vacation, as well as improper train- ing, can produce severe behavioral dis- turbances in your pet. These experiences, which affect the dog negatively, can trig- ger a great many symptoms of disease. As a rule, only an experienced behavioral therapist who specializes in treating ani- mals will be able to find the causes of the mental disturbance. He or she will try to "reprogram" the dog in the proper way. Ask your veterinarian for a referral.

HOW-TO:
Keeping Your Dog Healthy

If your pet should become ill, or if an emergency situation occurs, it is important to take a few important steps.

Visiting the Veterinarian

It is best to transport a sick dog to the veterinarian by car. Have someone ride with you to pet the dog and keep it calm.

You can help the veterinarian make a diagnosis by providing

1) Place tablets far back in the dog's mouth; then give it some water or moist food.

information about the dog's symptoms; therefore, you need to write down everything you have observed. Frequently, stool and urine samples will be helpful. Make a note of any medications you have given the dog, and remember to take along your pet's vaccination certificate.

Administering Medicine
Drawings 1 and 3

Tablets can be "concealed" in a piece of spreadable meat (such as liverwurst) or placed at the very back of the dog's tongue, while you hold its mouth open. Then hold its jaws shut until it swallows. Afterward, feed the dog something moist, to keep the tablet from getting stuck in its throat.

Liquid medications can be squirted into the side of the dog's mouth, between the rows of teeth, with a disposable plastic syringe (without the cannula, or tube). To do so, pull the dog's flews down slightly and raise its head.

Eye drops can be dripped behind the lower lid. Pull the lid slightly downward.

Eye ointment can be placed, in a ribbon, behind the upper eyelid. Carefully pull the lid upward.

Taking the Dog's Temperature
Drawing 2

Have someone familiar to the dog help you take its temperature. That person should hold it firmly around its neck and beneath its abdomen. Then you lift the dog's

2) Taking your dog's temperature is best done with a helper. Lubricate the thermometer first, and hold it still while the reading is being obtained.

tail and insert the thermometer, its tip lubricated with petroleum jelly, up to one third of its length into the dog's rectum. Hold the thermometer in place while the reading is being obtained, and talk to the dog soothingly to keep it calm. Practice this procedure from time to time while performing regular grooming.

Note: Shatterproof digital thermometers that beep to signal that the readout is ready are quite handy.

Home Medicine Chest
Instruments:
- one shatterproof thermometer
- one pair of curved scissors with one blunt blade and one sharp one
- one pair of scissors for cutting bandages
- one pair of tick tweezers
- one pair of tweezers with rounded tips
- two or three wooden spatulas to apply ointment
- three plastic syringes (without cannula) with a volume of 2 milliliters, 5 milliliters, and 10 milliliters, respectively, to administer medications, foods, or liquids.

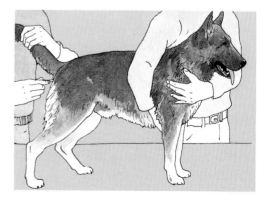

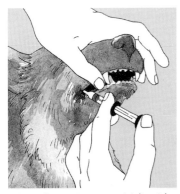

3) With a syringe, squirt liquid medications into one corner of the dog's mouth while you raise its head slightly.

Bandaging materials:
- elastic gauze bandages (2.4 and 4 inches [6 and 10 cm] wide)
- adhesive tape and Band-Aids
- surgical cotton
- gauze compresses
- one tourniquet bandage to stop bleeding.

Medications: There are no special medications or medical items—except the ones named above—necessary for a dog's medical kit. If in doubt regarding your dog's behavior, and possible illness, consult a veterinarian immediately! Handy for your first aid kit, however, are antiseptic solution, eyewash and an eyedropper, tweezers to remove splinters and such, a mercury rectal thermometer, petroleum jelly, and possibly an emergency snakebite kit.

Emergency Situations
Drawing 4

Now and then emergency situations can occur in which only quick action can save the life of your dog. Be aware of the following:

Insect sting: German shepherd dogs are very fond of snapping at wasps or bees, and sometimes they get stung. A sting in the mouth or throat can result in swelling that puts the dog's life in danger. If this should happen, cool its throat from the outside, by placing ice bags or ice cubes (in a sock or stocking) on its neck, and get your pet to the veterinarian posthaste! That also applies if the dog is stung several times by wasps, bees, or possibly a hornet on other parts of its body.

Cuts on the feet: While out for a walk, a dog can very easily step on a piece of broken glass or other sharp material. A gaping wound in the pad of its foot can result, and it will bleed profusely. If that occurs, make a pressure bandage at once. You may find someone with a first aid kit in the car who can provide you with a gauze compress and a bandage. Lay the compress directly on the injured area and wrap the bandage around it. In a pinch, a paper tissue will do the job: Place it on the wound and wrap a scrap of cloth around it. Then take the dog to the nearest veterinarian.

Bites: German shepherd dogs are apt to fight, and as a rule they do not seek to avoid a scuffle. If they do have a fight, have every bite examined by your veterinarian. The opponent's tooth will have made only a small, though often very deep, hole, and after a few days a serious infection can develop. Fever, apathy, loss of appetite, and blood poisoning can be the result.

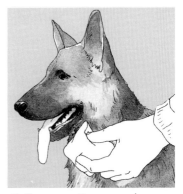

4) If a wasp stings your dog on the neck, hold an ice bag there to cool it.

Stanch heavily bleeding wounds with a pressure bandage, or use your hand to exert pressure on the blood vessel to keep the dog from bleeding to death. Get the dog to the veterinarian at once.

Poisoning: Symptoms of poisoning are heavy drooling, repeated vomiting with traces of blood, traces of blood in diarrhea and urine, pale to bluish mucous membranes, racing pulse, and/or loss of consciousness. See the veterinarian immediately!

If the veterinarian cannot be reached, the dog can still be helped 30 minutes to one hour after ingesting the poison by gastric irrigation with a solution of table salt (1 tablespoon of salt to 100 milliliters water). Force the solution down the dog's throat with a disposable syringe, minus the cannula. After the dog has vomited, give it as much water as possible to drink, to induce further vomiting. Call the Poison Control Center in your area.

Warning: If your dog has been poisoned, do not give it milk or oil.

Breed-related Diseases

There are certain diseases that are common to German shepherd dogs. Some of them are:

Hip dysplasia (HD): HD usually is a hereditary malformation that can appear in any dog of medium size or larger. Its incidence is greater when breeders fail to assure that parent animals (in preceding generations as well) are free of the malformation.

As affected young animals mature, this disease results in a poor fit between the acetabulum (cup) and the head of the femur (thigh bone). With increasing use (and overfeeding of the young dog), the joint suffers abnormal wear and tear, and premature arthritic changes develop. The dog's gait becomes waddling and swaying, it limps, experiences difficulty getting up and lying down, and finally is unable to move without pain.

Diagnosis can be made only by taking an X ray of the pelvis. Most pain medications that are given have serious side effects. Continuous use of cortisone decreases resistance. The most expensive—but most successful—treatment is insertion of an artificial hip joint. One new possibility is surgical correction of the malformed hip joint, which can be performed in dogs as young as six months.

Elbow dysplasia: The cause is a difference in the longitudinal growth of the ulna and the radius, caused by injuries at the growth sites. As a result, the joint articulates poorly, wears badly, and produces degenerative changes. This condition, developmental in origin, is very painful for the dog and is aggravated by excessive stress, such as during sports. Elbow dysplasia can appear in dogs as young as six to eight months. Surgery, if performed in time, can keep arthritic changes to a minimum.

Pancreatic insufficiency: This appears when the dog is one and one-half to two years old. The symptoms are weight loss despite voracious appetite; clay-colored stools, varying in softness, with an oily sheen; persistent digestive problems, occasional vomiting, flatulence, and diarrhea.

Gastric torsion: The symptoms are sudden bloating of the upper abdomen, restlessness, gagging, drooling, unsuccessful efforts to vomit, and difficulty breathing. Butyric acid fermentation causes the stomach to be drawn upward. The food-filled portion, however, sinks downward, which causes the stomach to rotate on its longitudinal axis. As a result of the additional filling with gas, the blood supply is interrupted as the vessels are strangulated. Death results in a few hours. When the first symptoms appear, contact the veterinarian at once; only surgery can help your pet.

Inflammation of the cornea (keratitis): The cornea is cloudy and smoky to milky in color. The inflammation can be caused by the presence of eyelashes or foreign bodies in the eye and a bacterial infection of the cornea. Small ulcers can develop in the cornea. If they break through the cornea, the inner part of the eye can flow out.

Cauda equina syndrome: This disease of the spine, which has been observed for some years in sporting dogs and working dogs, unfortunately affects German shepherd dogs as well. Since the working dog breeds are bred for extreme mobility, in the lumbar region in particular, the distance between the last lumbar vertebra and the first sacral vertebra—now genetically determined in quite a few dogs—is slightly larger than normal. When there is excessive stress, slippage of intervertebral disks can occur at this

Swimming in the summer strengthens a dog's physical condition and is good for its coat. It's fun too!

site, causing the dog great pain from pressure on the peripheral nerves of the spinal cord, which are bundled together into a "horsetail" (*cauda equina*) in roughly that place. The symptoms are: refusal to perform jump exercises or crying out in pain when jumping, lameness or weakness in the hindquarters, and/or sensitivity to pressure on the affected area. Since these symptoms are also characteristic of diseases in the hip area (HD), the problem frequently is misdiagnosed. An experienced specialist, however, can make an X-ray diagnosis after injecting a contrast medium into the spinal cord.

In the case of this spinal problem, an operation is often unavoidable. Conscientious dog owners should have their pet examined for a predisposition to this disease before beginning a demanding dog sport, at the same time the HD X ray is taken (when the dog is about one year old).

Breeding and Showing German Shepherd Dogs

Dog Breeding—a Serious Business

Breeding pure-bred dogs requires a great deal of expertise on the part of the breeder, as well as plenty of time and money. Exercise extreme care when choosing the parent animals, paying special attention to issues such as health and good character.

Puppies are cute, it's true, and it is understandable that you would like to see at least one litter of puppies grow up. But before you breed your female dog (bitch), you should be clear on a few points. Done the right way, dog breeding entails an enormous amount of time, money, room, and specialized knowledge. The idea is not to let your dog mate with the next best dog in the neighborhood, just because you subscribe to the ineradicable tradition that every female dog has to be a mother at least once in order to have a healthy, happy life. This assertion was refuted long ago. Animal shelters are full of mongrels without pedigrees that eke out a sad existence in "solitary confinement."

Only Selective Breeding Is Wise

Serious breeding has a clear goal: to maintain and improve the breed by strict selection of parent animals in regard to conformation, health, and strength of character. This sentence contains so much need for biological expertise, including a knowledge of genetics, and for responsibility toward the dog as a living creature, that even experienced breeders cannot always live up to these expectations.

Although the German shepherd dog is classified as one of the so-called utility (working) dog breeds, many breeders breed primarily for external features whose merits have long been controversial. A steep croup, as well as a "fastback" and excessive angulation of the hind limbs (see drawing, page 11) are allegedly what German shepherd dog fanciers desire (see The Breed Standard, page 10).

In high-performance sports, in police work, and in herding and guard work, German shepherd dogs with such a highly styled body are, in my experience, often not capable of holding up to stress for long, and have an increased incidence of muscle, tendon, and back problems, to mention only a few of the risks.

Beauty Alone?

True fanciers of this breed should not accept such products when they purchase a German shepherd dog; they should look not for beauty alone, but for physical health and a well-balanced character in the dog they buy. Tens of thousands of German shepherd dogs are bred annually—and not to order, as one can tell from the ads in the classified sections of many different newspapers. Who ends up with the puppies that "breeders" have to advertise for sale because no takers have been found? I witnessed dogs in unspeakable misery when I worked as a dog handler for the police force, taking part in efforts to prevent cruelty to animals. German shepherd dogs were caged in "solitary confinement" in junkyards, lying on short chains in the mud in front of leaky doghouses full of wet straw, and totally neglected animals that were fed only irregularly: and these are the least offensive examples! These poor dogs were given to someone frivolously by their breeders, with no follow-up supervision, either because they had produced too many of them, or because they didn't care what became of their overproduction.

Deviations from Breed Characteristics

In describing the breed characteristics, I have painted a picture of the ideal German shepherd dog. As we all know, however, we rarely find reality measuring up to our ideals. Judged in terms of breed standards, many dog will show at least small "faults" that are difficult, if not impossible, to detect in a puppy, but that become all too evident in the adult dog. If your dog should prove to have some major faults—something that you might never become aware of unless you enter it in a show—do not take out your disappointment on your dog, who is not to blame for the breed standards. All that really matters is your dog's devotion to you.

Anything that negatively affects the dog's endurance, ability to perform, or capacity for work is considered a fault, as is an overall appearance unsuitable to a male or female. Apathy, nervousness, shyness, and lack of vitality are undesirable. A few physical faults are extreme paleness of the coat, albinism, the lack of one or both testicles in a male, exceeding or falling below standard measurements, underdeveloped parts of the body, legs that are too short or too long, weak jaws or jaws that are too long or too short, overshot or undershot jaw, too long, too short, or too soft a coat, flop ears, a curly or bent tail, and too short a tail.

Dog Shows

Every year there are local and regional shows for German shepherd dogs. Using the breed standards as a basis, the judges evaluate and grade dogs on their general appearance, physique, bearing, and behavior. Apart from the evaluation of the dogs, dog shows offer a wealth of information. Manufacturers of dog foods offer samples of the latest brands, usually at little or no cost. Useful accessories for dog owners are also on display. Contacts with other dog owners are quickly formed, and there is always a lively exchange of experience and information. The judges give tips and suggestions for the care and grooming of your dog.

If you would like to enter your dog in a show, check your club publications for dates and send in your application (available from the German Shepherd Club of America) and entry fee in plenty of time. Before the judging, you will have to supply the judges with your dog's pedigree, certificate of health (the local public health authorities often require this, too), and the International

In this way, the mother dog stimulates her puppy's digestive processes.

Certificate of Immunization. For further details, inquire at your German shepherd dog club. Do not go to the show expecting your dog to win a prize or even to come off with a particularly good evaluation—the judges are very strict and often stingy with prizes!

Servicing

To be on the safe side when breeding, you need to have your brood bitch examined "from stem to stern" by the veterinarian before you have her serviced by a male, to make absolutely sure that she is in good health.

Stud: As a rule, the owner of a brood bitch does not keep his or her own stud, but looks for another breeder with a suitable partner. Consult an experienced breeder (one from your club, for example) when you are ready to select the male. The national champion is not always the best choice for your bitch. Talk to the male's owner before the servicing occurs to agree on the stud fee (approximately the selling price of a puppy) and arrange the other formalities, such as, inspection of the papers.

This curious puppy explores its surroundings.

The Estrus Cycle

Normally a bitch comes into heat, or estrus, twice a year. The intervals can shift by several months, however, for a variety of reasons. If you know your bitch well, you will realize when the right time has come.

The first heat of a female dog occurs when she is about eight months old. After that she comes into heat regularly, approximately every six months. The estrus cycle has three phases and lasts roughly three weeks: *proestrus* (the first 10 days), *estrus* (days 10 to 16), and *diestrus* (a few days).

During the first 10 days of the cycle, the vulva begins to swell and the bitch bleeds slightly. She will bite importunate males to keep them away. Nevertheless, the first day of the bleeding is important for calculating the servicing day: It will be the eleventh to sixteenth day after the onset of bleeding. The veterinarian can take a vaginal swab to determine the right time for servicing.

During the peak phase, or estrus, the bloody discharge turns pink, indicating that the bitch is ready to mate. During the diestrus phase, the swelling of the bitch's vulva subsides, and her behavior returns to normal.

The Mating Act

The bitch is always brought to the stud. It is important that you allow natural love play to occur between the two dogs. Make no attempt to force the bitch to mate by holding her still or putting a muzzle on her. If she rejects the male, it is either the wrong day or nature is just having its way.

Do not select a "novice" stud when your bitch is to be serviced for the first time. When the male mounts the female, it may be necessary to calm down the novice bitch, if the stud

A puppy quickly learns passive submission from its mother.

allows it. After the penis is inserted, the male's bulbus glandis (a section of the penis) swells and the bitch's vaginal ring constricts; the dogs are "tied" together. This may last anywhere from ten minutes to just under one hour. The male may shift his position so that he and the female are positioned rear to rear until the muscles relax. When the tie is prolonged, and if the weather is hot, give the dogs fresh water to drink. Forcefully separating them could seriously injure the bitch. Even after the mating has taken place, keep the bitch at home under a certain amount of supervision, until she resumes biting males to chase them away.

Gestation

The bitch will give birth, or whelp, on the sixty-third day after being serviced.

Gestation periods of as few as 58 or as many as 65 days are not uncommon, however, if the bitch continues to behave normally and her temperature does not exceed 102.2°F (39°C).

At this time, the bitch needs high-energy, top-quality foods. Feed her two or three times a day. Do not let her put on too much weight, however, or she will have difficulty giving birth.

Until the fifth week of pregnancy, she may continue to move around as usual. From then on, however, although she needs plenty of exercise outdoors, she should no longer engage in sports, including activities such as jumping, climbing, or running alongside your bike. In winter, do not let her swim in cold water. From the fifth week on, give her additional vitamins and minerals, as your veterinarian advises. From the seventh week on you will be able to feel the puppies move. Give the bitch excellent care, by brushing and drying her after a walk in the rain and by giving her daily cuddling and physical contact (see page 22). Such measures will stimulate her circulation, as well as cell growth, and benefit the puppies as well.

The Whelping Box

Equipment: For a large animal like the German shepherd dog, the whelping box needs to measure at least 48 inches (120 cm) × 40 inches (100 cm), with a height of 16 inches (40 cm). Cover the bottom of the box with a thick layer of newspapers, and place an old sheet on top of them. Collect newspapers and old linens ahead of time; you will need more of them than you think.

Location: The whelping box should be set up in a quiet, draft-free area in your home. Choose a room where you also can sleep the last few nights before the expected birth.

Note: Set up the box at least two weeks before the expected due date and encourage the bitch to sleep in it so that she will get used to it.

The puppy licks the corner of its mother's mouth to tell her it wants to be fed.

Labor and Delivery

About one week before the expected due date, start to check the bitch's temperature daily. About the sixty-first or sixty-second day, the temperature suddenly will plunge to about 99°F or below (36.5°C). Now the birth is imminent; it will occur within the next 24 to 72 hours. Shortly before giving birth, the bitch usually will "dig" around in the newspapers inside her whelping box. This is normal. From now on, do not leave her alone.

Once the bitch starts to bear down and a mucous discharge becomes visible, the first puppy is about to make its appearance—nicely packaged in an amniotic sac. The bitch uses her teeth to bite open the sac and sever the umbilical cord. She eats the amniotic sac and the afterbirth (placenta). (Do not let her eat more than one in order to prevent diarrhea.) Then she licks the newborn dry, thus stimulating its circulation. Normally, a puppy will be born every 10 to 45 minutes. If the bitch continues to press down unsuccessfully for more than 45 minutes, call the veterinarian. If she is unable or unwilling to bite open the amniotic sac, you will have to do that for her with your fingernails, so that the puppy's head is free and it can breathe. Massage the umbilical cord toward the puppy's body, and use your fingernails to pinch off the umbilical cord about 0.8 inch (2 cm) away from its abdomen. Tie it with dental floss, then cut it.

As soon as their mother has licked them clean, the puppies should begin their determined search for the milk source, her teats. For good reason, the bitch offers them no help in their struggle. A puppy that cannot manage to find its way to the teats unassisted will not be a healthy, vital dog later on. In the wild, the bitch would let it die, because it is not capable of surviving. Make a note of each puppy's time of birth and weight. You will need to weigh them every day, to keep track of their development. The day after the birth, have your bitch examined by the veterinarian, to make sure that there is not a puppy still in her womb.

My tip: Make arrangements with the veterinarian ahead of time, so that he or she is on call when the birth is near.

The Development of the Puppies

The puppies are blind and deaf when born, but they have a full coat of hair.

Weight: At birth they weigh about 16 to 19 ounces (450–550 g). The first few weeks they gain 8 to 10 percent (about 1.7 ounces, or 50 g) of their own weight daily. In the second month of life, the daily weight gain should amount to 20 to 25 percent (about 3.5 ounces, or 100 g).

Keeping the puppies clean: The mother dog herself takes care of "changing the diapers." She uses her tongue to massage the puppies' bellies regularly, and in this way stimulates their digestive processes. She consumes their feces, and whatever urine she fails to catch will trickle down into the layers of newspaper. The newspapers, along with the sheet covering them, have to be changed regularly.

About the tenth or twelfth day of life, the puppies' eyes slowly open. Their hearing also develops bit by bit.

From the third week on, the teeth erupt through the gums.

From the fourth week on, the puppies are already trying to get out of the whelping box to explore their surroundings. Place a skidproof rubber mat under the sheet in the whelping box, so that the puppies do not slip as they begin to be active.

In the fourth to seventh weeks, you, as the breeder, bear a great responsibility. The puppies are in the socialization and imprinting phase (see page 20). They now need continuous skin contact with humans. You have to spend time with the puppies and pet them on a daily basis. From the fourth or fifth week on, you also can allow children to play with the puppies—under your supervision. If you have other pets, start getting the little puppies accustomed to them now. During the socialization phase, the puppies practice important behavioral patterns with their siblings, often in tempestuous games.

In the eighth week, the puppies will have a number tattooed on the inside of one ear before they go to new homes. The tattooed number is recorded in the certificate of origin (see page 15).

Feeding the Puppies

From roughly the third to fourth week onward—depending on how many puppies there are—you need to slowly begin feeding them solid foods. While the bitch is feeding her puppies herself, continue to give her at least twice her usual amount of high-energy food, with vitamin and mineral supplements as the veterinarian advises.

Now, very slowly begin to switch the puppies to a new diet. Give them puppy-rearing milk, fresh finely-ground raw beef with cereal flakes, or special, nutritionally complete puppy food. If you decide on commercial puppy food, do not feed the puppies any additional vitamins and minerals; everything they need is contained in the puppy food. Ask an experienced breeder ahead of time what to feed puppies over eight weeks old.

Index

*Two dogs meet:
After nose contact
is established, an
anal check follows.*

Useful Addresses and Literature

International Kennel Clubs

As an address is almost invariably the home of an officer of the breed club, it is understandable that it can change as elections are held. It is wise to check with the American Kennel Club (AKC), 51 Madison Avenue, New York, NY 10038 for an update on a club's address.

German Shepherd Club of America
17 Ivy Lane
Englewood, New Jersey 07631

American Kennel Club (AKC)
51 Madison Avenue
New York, New York 10038

Australian Kennel Club
Royal Show Ground
Ascot Vale
Victoria, Australia

Canadian Kennel Club
89 Skyway Avenue
Etovicoke, Ontario M9W6R4

Fédération Internationale
Cynologique (FCI)
13 Place Albert I,
B-6530 Thuin
Belgium

The Kennel Club
1-4 Clargis Street, Piccadilly
London W7Y 8AB
England

New Zealand Kennel Club
P.O. Box 523
Wellington, 1
New Zealand

Verein für Deutsche Schäferhunde
e.v. (SV)
D-86167 Augsburg
Germany

Information and Printed Material

American Boarding Kennel
Association
4575 Galley Road, Suite 400 A
Colorado Springs, Colorado 80915
(Publishes lists of approved boarding kennels.)

American Society for the Prevention
of Cruelty to Animals (ASPCA)
441 East 92nd Street
New York, New York 10128

American Veterinary Medical
Association
930 North Meacham Road
Schaumberg, Illinois 60173

Gaines TWT
P.O. Box 8172
Kankakee, Illinois 60901
(Publishes *Touring with Towser,* a directory of hotels and motels that accommodate guests with dogs.)

Humane Society of the United States
(HSUS)
2100 L Street NW
Washington, DC 20037

Books

In addition to the most recent edition of the official publication of the American Kennel Club, *The Complete Dog Book*, published by Howell Book House, New York, other suggestions include:

Alderton, David, *The Dog Care Manual.* Hauppauge, New York: Barron's Educational Series, Inc., 1986.

Antesberger, Helmut, *The German Shepherd Dog.* Hauppauge, New York: Barron's Educational Series, Inc., 1985.

Baer, Ted, *Communicating with Your Dog.* Hauppauge, New York: Barron's Educational Series, Inc., 1989.

___, *How to Teach Your Old Dog New Tricks.* Hauppauge, New York: Barron's Educational Series, Inc., 1991.

Klever, Ulrich, *The Complete Book of Dog Care.* Hauppauge, New York: Barron's Educational Series, Inc., 1989.

Ullmann, Hans, *The New Dog Handbook.* Hauppauge, New York: Barron's Educational Series, Inc., 1984.

Wrede, Barbara, *Civilizing Your Puppy.* Hauppauge, New York: Barron's Educational Series, Inc., 1992.

The Cover Photos

Front cover: Male, short hair, black and tan, Key von Aurelius.
Back cover: Female, long hair, black and tan, with eight-week-old puppy.

Important Note

This pet owner's guide tells the reader how to buy and care for a German shepherd dog. The author and the publisher consider it important to point out that the guidelines presented in this book apply primarily to normally developed young animals from a reputable breeder—that is, to dogs in excellent physical health and of good character.

Anyone who adopts an adult dog should be aware that it may already have been substantially influenced by other human beings. You must keep a close eye on such a dog, including its behavior toward humans. Be sure to meet the previous owner as well. If the dog comes from an animal shelter, someone there may be able to give you information about the dog's origin and peculiarities. Some dogs have behavioral problems due to bad experiences with humans; they may also have a tendency to bite. Such animals should be adopted only by experienced dog owners.

Even with well-trained, carefully supervised dogs, there is a possibility that they will damage someone else's property or, even worse, cause accidents. It is in your own interest to purchase adequate insurance coverage, and, in any event, we strongly urge you to take out a liability insurance policy that covers the dog.

In addition, see that your dog has all the necessary immunizations and worm treatments; otherwise, the health of humans and animals is at considerable risk. Some diseases and parasites can be transmitted to humans. If your dog exhibits symptoms of illness, it is essential to consult a veterinarian. If you have questions about your own health, see your physician.

About the Author

Horst Hegewald-Kawich, long employed as a dog handler by the police, has for many years conducted imprinting play days for puppies and adult dogs. He serves as a judge at dog sports tournaments and an examiner of dogs trained to work with the blind. He also has had many years of experience in dealing with problem dogs.

About the Illustrator

György Jankovics, trained as a graphic artist, studied at the Art Academy of Budapest and the Hamburg Academy of Arts. He draws animal and plant subjects for a number of prominent European publishing houses, and has illustrated a great many books.

About the Photographer

Monika Wegler is a professional photographer, journalist, and author of books about animals. In the past few years, the focus of her work has been portraits of animals, as well as behavioral studies and motion studies of dogs and cats.

All inquiries should be addressed to:
Barron's Educational Series, Inc.
250 Wireless Boulevard
Hauppauge, NY 11788

International Standard Book No. 0-8120-9749-1

Library of Congress Catalog Card No. 96-20188

Library of Congress Cataloging-in-Publication Data
Hegewald-Kawich, Horst.
   [*Der deutsche Schäferhund.* English]
   The German shepherd dog : everything about purchase, care, nutrition, breeding, and training / Horst Hegewald-Kawich ; consulting editor, Matthew M. Vriends.
      p.   cm. — (A Complete pet owner's manual)
   Includes bibliographical references (p. 62) and index.
   ISBN 0-8120-9749-1
   1. German shepherd dogs. I. Vriends, Matthew M., 1937–
II. Title. III. Series.
SF429.G37H4413   1996
636.7'37—dc20   96-20188
                                              CIP

Printed in Hong Kong

987654321

In the summer this German shepherd dog races through the water exuberantly. But it is never allowed to step or jump into the water unless directed to do so, because dangers, such as pieces of glass, can lurk in strange waters. Also, in flooded gravel pits that are not yet open to the public, there often are iron structures still concealed under the surface that can seriously injure the dog when it leaps into the water.